ALLEN RIDER GUIDES

RIDING TO MUSIC

ALLEN RIDER GUIDES

Riding to Music

Janet W. Macdonald

J. A. Allen

London

For the Simmons family in memory of Lad — the Black Knight's horse and the star of the show; and for Sonia Burt, who made the whole thing possible.

British Library Cataloguing in Publishing Data

A catalogue record for this book is available from the British Library

ISBN−0−85131−567−4

Published in Great Britain in 1987 by
J. A. Allen & Company Limited,
1, Lower Grosvenor Place, Buckingham Palace Road,
London, SW1W 0EL

© Janet W. Macdonald, 1987

Second Edition 1992

Text cartoons by Ann Pilgrim
Text design by Nancy Lawrence

Contents

— Contents —

List of Illustrations

List of Cartoons

Acknowledgements

My grateful thanks to the following for all their help: Messrs Wilson and Powis at Philips Electrical, for information on Compact Disc; Bernard Stringer for editing *Wintersturmer* and showing me how to do it; Deirdre Robinson for information on quadrilles, Sarah Whitmore for information on dressage; Jean Sansom at the BHS for information on dressage competitions, Ken Maxwell-Jones, ex P.T.I. and Royal Tournament team coach; and the many ladies who told me of their competitive experiences.

Introduction

Riding to music is not a new concept. The old court riding schools of Europe used to put on displays for their patrons, which often included what they called a 'ballet'. Like the ballet we know today, the story was enacted to music, but the performers were mounted on highly-schooled horses. Although they do not perform ballets, the Spanish Riding School of Vienna carry on this tradition of displays to music which delight audiences all over the world.

A newer development is the 'Freestyle to Music' dressage competitions which are gaining popularity. The most famous of these in Britain is held at Goodwood as part of the National Championships. Here the test includes all the Grand Prix movements and for spectators it is probably the most popular of all the tests. But you do not have to have a highly-schooled horse to ride to music. There are dressage competitions at lower levels, side-saddle and hack competitions, and the annual Riding Clubs Quadrille competition. Clubs with their own message to impart, such as the Side-Saddle Association (SSA) (see Useful Addresses), frequently produce musical displays.

Music is an excellent teaching and schooling aid, especially in situations where regular rhythm has been a problem, or where a nervous rider is passing her nervousness to the horse. Music can help solve these and other problems.

There is no reason why you should not ride to music for the sheer fun of doing so. At a time when places to ride freely out of doors are becoming more and more restricted, it is easy for the non-competitive rider to become bored in a manege. In

Professional ...

... and amateur

this situation, music can add another infinitely changeable dimension. You do not even have to know anything about music. Crotchets and quavers, minims and semi-breves are all irrelevant. What matters is rhythm and beat.

For the person who wants to ride to music for pure enjoyment, all that is needed is a horse and a means of playing music. For the competitively inclined, add a stopwatch (and an assistant to operate it and take notes) and a metronome.

(Please note that I have referred throughout to riders as 'she' and horses as 'he'. This is in the interests of clarity, not for any sexist motive.)

1

Sound Reproduction Equipment

Cassette Players

Now, and for the foreseeable future, the best method of sound reproduction is by tape cassette. There are other developments taking place in the most secret depths of manufacturers' research laboratories, notably DAT (Digital Audio Tape) which works on the same principle as compact disc but will allow you to record as well as play. However, it will be some years before it is as universally available as cassettes and cassette players.

Spare cassettes can be carried in a pocket and battery-operated players come in a variety of sizes, many light enough and small enough to be carried by a mounted rider. If you are working out of doors on your own, the ubiquitous 45-gallon oil drum makes a convenient place for the cassette player to stand, and is high enough to reach from even the tallest horse. These drums do not cause a noticeable difference in sound quality.

It should go without saying that wherever you stand the player, it should be out of reach of hooves and inquisitive noses, especially if the 'Record' button is reachable by such a nose. If you have nowhere to stand the player, the alternative is to hang it over a fence post or convenient tree. Unlike record players, cassette players will operate perfectly well suspended or propped at angles. They can also, of course, be placed on a conveniently located car and can be wired into the car battery if extra volume is needed. For most purposes, the average portable player will produce enough sound to cover 30 m

Do not turn it on suddenly at full volume

so as long as you place it halfway along your working area you will be able to hear adequately without upsetting the neighbours.

Cassette players built into cars are not really practicable, for several reasons. Quite apart from the problem of getting the car close enough to your working area, especially after rain, you will need an assistant to operate the player. You will also have to have all the windows/doors/roof of the car open to allow the sound out and will need the volume very high, for the speakers are normally located to aim the sound at the occupants of the car, not those outside it. Built-in car cassette players rarely have tape counters, so it will not be easy to locate a specific track, and some of them have a nasty habit of mangling tapes.

DUST, RAIN AND TEMPERATURE   No music reproduction device, nor the tapes (or records) will function for long if exposed to moisture or dust, so care must be taken to avoid these. The simplest and cheapest solution to the problem is to put the player in a plastic bag. This does not noticeably affect the quality or amount of sound and it allows the operator to see and operate the controls without removing the protective cover. A 'Head-cleaning' tape should be used more frequently than with a domestic player and the cassettes themselves should always be replaced in their box immediately or they will attract dust.

Modern equipment is not unduly temperature sensitive, but should not be exposed to freezing nor left in bright summer sunshine for long periods. It will also attract condensation brought on by constantly fluctuating temperatures in damp places, so it is not wise to leave cassette players in unheated tack rooms or indoor schools.

Permanent installations in indoor schools are best done by experts who will advise on siting for speakers as well as protective cabinets for both players and cassettes/discs. These will operate off the normal electricity supply, but should not be wired in to a coin-metered supply with an abrupt cut-off.

COST   A perfectly adequate portable cassette player can be purchased for little more than the cost of shoeing a horse, although for this price you will not get stereo.

Blank cassettes are quite inexpensive, with the actual price depending on the length of play (30, 45 or 60 minutes per side) and the quality and type of the coating. Do buy cassettes from a reputable manufacture − alternatives may be a lot cheaper, but tend to be inadequately coated and mounted on poor spools which soon fail.

The price of pre-recorded music depends on the popularity of the performers. If you want a specific *piece* of music rather than a particular artist/orchestra, and the tempo is not different, it pays to shop around the chain-store 'own label' recordings.

Why prevent your horse hearing the music?

Personal Stereos

These are very useful when you are looking for a suitable piece of music. The ideal situation for listening to them is during a brisk walk; if you cannot move your own feet regularly and evenly to a piece of music, it is unlikely that you will be able to persuade a horse to do so. Personal stereos are invaluable when you or your team members are learning a piece for a performance or competition, for you will soon drive your family mad if you play the same piece of music out loud over and over again.

Whether personal stereos are appropriate for mounted use is another matter. Most of them do not have a suitable carrying case and if you carry them in a pocket, a brisk trot or the occasional buck/nap, etc. is likely to pull the ear-phone plug out or operate the switches. There is also the problem of keeping the ear-phones in place comfortably, especially under a riding hat. But anyway, why prevent your horse hearing the music? Most of them like it and will adjust their gaits to the tempo, so unless you fear equine anticipation in a crucial competition, there is little point in keeping the sound to yourself.

Compact Disc

There are portable compact disc players, although they cost a lot more than portable cassette players. Although remote control devices are not available for portable players at the time of writing, manufacturers are working on types which will fit easily into a pocket and operate up to 30 m from the player. The discs themselves play for up to 80 minutes and, like cassettes, are all a standard size and play at a standard speed. At the time of writing you cannot record onto compact discs, but manufacturers are working on this facility. Probably the greatest value with compact disc lies in its use as an editing device.

Recording onto Cassettes

If you want to ride *to* music, rather than ride with a musical background, you are immediately faced with the problem of finding adequate quantities of suitable music. With the exception of special cassettes (Chapter 3), most records or cassettes are not compiled with the rider in mind and there will only be one or two suitable tracks on any given album. You will therefore need to copy what you want on to your own cassette. For this you will need a 'music centre', which will cost between a couple of hundred pounds and several thousand, depending on the degree of sophistication and the quality of sound reproduction you desire. For straightforward copying from record to cassette, the cheapest version will do.

All you need do is put in a blank cassette, put a record on the turntable, press 'Record' and stand by to press 'Stop' at the end of the track you are recording. It is sensible to set the counter to zero when starting and to make a note of the counter reading on the cassette label. Do be sure the record you are copying from is not warped or scratched, or the noises this causes will also form part of your recording.

Editing

Competition rules specify a set time for your performance. Recorded music unfortunately rarely conforms to these times, so it is necessary to remove chunks if the piece you want is too long, or put two or more pieces of music together on the cassette if they are too short. You can do this with the basic equipment described above, but unless you are able to press buttons with split-second timing there will inevitably be gaps or unwanted noises on your recording.

What professional music editors do is to record the whole piece on to reel-to-reel tape, physically cut out the unwanted portions with a razor blade, splice the tape back together and then record the result back onto cassette. It requires considerable technical expertise, because you have to actually cut the right place of the right note, so you need to know the precise speed of your tape to measure centimetres to cut. It is better to cross-fade or mix, but for this you need at least two tape machines, locked together in synchronisation.

Unless you have access to such expertise, you need a rather more sophisticated music centre or hi-fi stack. These can be put together in any format you want, to allow you to copy from a record, cassette or compact disc, but the main requirement is a 'Pause' button on the recorder. This allows you to stop the recordings smoothly and hold it in pause while you find the next piece you want and then to release it equally smoothly without a nasty 'bonk' on the recording. What you may be prepared to put up with at home will be an intolerable intrusion when it is played over loudspeakers. Don't forget that bad sound reproduction will offend a knowledgeable audience.

Whichever way you do it, you must always stop or start each piece at the end (or beginning) of a bar. You must make your own aesthetic judgements of which music to mix, but do aim for smooth transitions from piece to piece, with matching sound levels and tones. As a general principle it is wise to stick to the same instrument or group of instruments — don't jump from a haunting violin to a honky-tonk piano. Quite apart from the shock it will give your audience, it is rare that such a radical change of mood suits the paces of the horse.

Do use a stopwatch to time your finished piece and adjust it if necessary. You will probably have to ride through it and adjust it several times before it is right, but do not be tempted to skimp on this chore, for it will be obvious to observers.

One of the advantages of using compact disc to record from is the flexibility of this system. Because the disc is read by a laser, it can jump from one place to another on the disc very quickly. Also, each minute portion of the disc has a specified location and the players have such detailed counters that you can identify each note on the disc. You can programme the players to find any note you want; to start playing from that note and stop at another; to jump over a section and play on; to play designated sections in any order you want; or to repeat any section as many times as you want. And you can do it all by remote control if you wish.

This sophisticated 'programmability' is marvellous if you cannot find quite the piece of music you want. For instance, perhaps you want to do two-time flying changes all the way down the middle of the arena, which takes 15 seconds, but the piece of music you like only has 5 seconds of suitable music. All you have to do is set the programmer to play the 5 second phase twice more before carrying on with the rest of the music.

Once you have your piece of music as you want it, do not forget to make at least one copy in case of disasters. It would be a pity to lose the results of all your work.

2

Legalities and Licences

Chapter 1 was the good news on all the things you can do with modern technology. Here is the bad news — you are not allowed to do any of it, except play a purchased pre-recorded disc, tape or record for your own private use, or have a member of your family play a musical instrument, again for your own private use.

Or rather, you are not allowed to do it without various licences and permissions. If you do, you will be laying yourself open to prosecution for infringing 'copyright'.

Copyright

Most people think of copyright as relating to books and the written word, but it also applies to music and sound recordings. Where the actual music is concerned, copyright begins with the creation of the patterns of notes themselves — so you could technically be infringing copyright by just whistling a tune in the street. Then there is also copyright in printed and recorded music.

Such copyright normally belongs to the person who created the piece of music (unless the piece was commissioned, in which case it might belong to the commissioner, depending on the terms under which it was commissioned) but the law considers it to be actual property. So, like any other property, it can be sold, leased, lent, hired or left in a will to somebody else.

Copyright normally belongs to the composer for his lifetime and 50 years after his death. However, if the music had not been performed or published in that lifetime, copyright runs for 50 years after the first performance or publication. After that time, the copyright runs out and anyone may use the music without permission.

'ARRANGEMENTS' You might think that you would be safe using a piece of Mozart that you know was performed publicly in his lifetime. After all, he's been dead more than 50 years. But are you sure the piece you intend to use is exactly as it was originally written? If it is not, you could still be infringing copyright, for the piece may have been 'arranged' by another composer, who then holds the copyright on that arrangement for the 50 year period as above.

You may not, yourself, make an arrangement of a piece of music without the permission of the copyright owner, nor may you make any other sort of adaptation.

RECORDING You may not record music from a live performance without the permission of the copyright owner and the consent of the performer. Both should be obtained in writing or by licence.

PUBLIC PERFORMANCES Nor may you give, or cause to be given, a public performance of a piece of music without permission. 'Public Performance' means *anything* outside your family or immediate domestic circle. So using music as a teaching aid is a public performance; and so are performances for members of a club, even if entrance is restricted to 'members only, no guests'. Certainly any performance in a place where the general public can walk in and watch/listen comes under the prohibited heading; whether or not the observers are charged an admission fee; whether or not the performers are paid; and whether or not the performance is for charity. (Don't forget we are discussing a piece of property, whose owner may not wish to make a contribution to that particular charity.) Rehearsals are not generally considered performances, unless open to an audience.

Responsibility for Copyright Infringement _____

Infringements of copyright, if detected, are usually dealt with by the owners of the copyright obtaining a High Court injunction against the offenders, which specifically forbids any further offences. Ignoring such an injunction is considered contempt of court, which is a criminal offence and could lead to a prison sentence or fine.

The copyright owners will probably be awarded damages and costs against you. (The company that the author works for obtained a High Court injunction in 1985 — the legal costs were over £1,500.)

The promoters of a public performance (and that could include the members of a riding club committee or a team coach), the owners of the premises used for that performance, and the performers, can all be held responsible for copyright infringements. So, if you are in any of those positions, do be sure the necessary permissions and licences have been obtained, or you could find yourself having to foot a large bill. And don't think that if there are a lot of you involved, you will only be liable for a share of the costs — the liability is 'joint and several' which means that if anyone cannot pay their share, the others involved must do so.

The music industry used to turn a blind eye to individuals infringing copyright, but they don't any more. They have got quite annoyed about it, especially copying and editing of recorded music, and are actively looking for infringements. You may think that the individual composers and musicians will not go to the trouble and expense of sueing you and you are right. They will not do it themselves, they will get the societies that represent them to do it and they can be very nasty indeed. Once they have won their case against you (and ignorance is no defence) they will make sure they collect the money that is due, even if they have to take you to the bankruptcy courts. You have been warned!

Getting Permission _____

You may be horrified at the idea of having to track down a

series of composers, arrangers, copyright owners and recording artists to get the permissions you need but it is actually quite easy. They are dealt with by PRS (The Performing Right Society), PPL (Phonographic Performances Ltd), or MCPS (Mechanical Copyright Protection Society); you should address letters or telephone enquiries to 'The Licencing Department' of these organisations. (See Useful Addresses.)

The Performing Right Society

This society represents only the composers and publishers of music (not performers) by granting you a licence on their behalf. This licence does *not* cover you for the use of the sound recording. For that you need an *additional* licence from PPL. (Yes — *two* separate licences to use recorded music.)

PRS operate a tariff system for licence charges. If they catch you using music when you haven't a licence, they make a 50 per cent surcharge. They usually provide a licence on an annual basis, but will provide permits on a one-off basis, either for owners of premises or organisers of events, where such events are not normally held. For the normal riding club or demonstration organiser, the cost of a blanket licence is so cheap (around the cost of having one horse shod) that it is silly not to get the licence. You do not need to specify the music you intend to use, just tell them how many performances you expect to give in the year. At the end of the year, you tell them how many you did give, and they will adjust the cost of next year's licence if you didn't pay enough. They may ask for the size of the venue, by which they mean the number of spectators.

Incidentally, if you are performing at a major show, especially one that is televised, you may be approached by someone with a clipboard who will ask you for details of your music (i.e. which pieces and what duration). Do not worry about this — your performance will be covered by the show's licence, but the PRS needs detailed information to know how much to distribute to the composers whose music has been played.

PRS has contracts with all the foreign rights societies, so your licence from them covers you for music written by foreign as well as British composers.

Using Live Musicians

If you do not wish to obtain more than one licence (the one from PRS) you will have to use live musicians. Wherever you find them, you should not assume that they are authorised to perform any piece of music (e.g. a relative of the composer). You must still get that licence.

There are many sources for finding amateur musicians. Ask your family, friends or riding club. Ask at your local library; they will know which schools have a good band or orchestra or whether there is a local music club that can help. Just be sure that whoever you choose is proficient enough to maintain a regular tempo from one session to another.

If you would prefer to use professional musicians, start by asking your Regional Arts Council for help. If your local library does not know the address, contact the Arts Council of Great Britain. (See Useful Addresses.) They will give advice on performers and they are usually keen to help young artists, which means a lower fee. There is a faint chance that they

Give serious thought to where you will situate live musicians

could give you some financial help, but only a very faint chance as this aid is normally reserved for public non-profit-making concerts.

The Incorporated Society of Musicians (see Useful Addresses) produces a list of professional musicians called 'The Professional Register of Artists'.

The British Music Year Book (in your local library) lists artists' agents, orchestras and colleges or schools of music who will supply information about those of their students whom they feel would benefit from performing experience.

Whenever you find your musicians, you will need to give some serious thought to exactly where to situate them. This may not be easy in an indoor manege; for example, if it is above the arena the sound may not carry all round the school from the gallery. The horses may be alarmed by large instruments, or light reflected from them, and the musicians will not thank you for subjecting their precious instruments to a damp or dusty environment.

Commissioning a Special Piece of Music _____

If you are put off by the business of obtaining licences, or by the complications of editing music to fit your time requirements, and of obtaining the permission to edit (see below) you may feel you would like to find a composer to write you a special piece of music. All you need is to ensure that your contract with the composer (and the actual contract can be as simple as a letter saying 'This is what we agreed, please sign the copy and return it to me.') states that you have the right of first performance. They cannot assign all rights to you — once they join PRS, they assign all rights to PRS, including past ones.

Finding a willing and affordable composer is not as difficult as you might think. If you cannot find a suitable one in the British Music Year Book, ask the British Academy of Songwriters, Composers and Authors (BASCA) to suggest some. (See Useful Addresses.)

There are two good reasons why a young composer will be delighted to work for you. The first is that many of them aspire to write the very lucrative pieces of music needed for films, television and advertising, which have to be timed to the split second. A three, five or six minute piece is easy for them, but excellent practise. The second reason is connected with PRS, which distributes the revenue from those blanket licences to its members, which include composers. Among the requirements for membership is a category which requires them to have had a certain number of works performed in public a certain number of times. The piece you want may be just what the composer needs to qualify for this membership, and they will be extra keen if there is a chance of your performance at a major show being televised.

Using Recorded Music

Recorded music is subject to a second type of copyright on the actual recording, as distinct from the copyright in the music itself. The PRS licence does not cover this type of copyright (which lasts for 50 years from the publication of the recording) so if you are intending to use recorded music, whether tapes, cassettes, discs or records, you need a licence from PPL *as well as* from PRS. This applies to teaching as well as performances.

PPL is a company which was formed to administer licences for sound recordings. Its members are the producers and record companies who have assigned their rights to PPL, so you must apply to PPL in the first instance. If the piece you want to use has not been assigned to them, they will be able to tell you who to contact instead. PPL has international licencing agreements with most foreign record producers, as imported recordings are still under copyright.

Like PRS, PPL gives a blanket licence, usually on an annual basis, with the cost calculated on a tariff basis. You do not need to list all the recordings you intend to use, but you do need to tell them the length of the music, the number of performances to be given in the year, the number of venues used and the size of the audience.

Copying of Recordings

As far as the music industry is concerned, copying a recording, known as re-recording, is the most heinous crime, unless, of course, you have permission and have paid a fee. MCPS will help you to obtain this permission, either by providing you with a licence itself, or by putting you in touch with the publisher or record company. (In the latter case, you write to the 'Legal Department' of the company.) In come cases, you may also need permission from the artist's agent.

If you are planning to make a compilation of pieces, it is obviously going to be easier applying for permission if all the pieces you want to use are from one recording company. However, do not assume that permission will be granted automatically. Where popular pieces are concerned, there may already be a contract between the original publisher and a compilation company (such as KTel), that specifically prohibits permission being given to anyone else.

MCPS will provide a basic licence. You write to them with details of the composer, the name of the piece of music, the performers, the record number, what you intend to use it for, how many times, and the size of the audience. Give them a telephone number and they will call you with a price. If you agree, they will send you an invoice with the licence. This basic licence is personal to the named person or club. It does not allow you to lend or hire your copied music to anyone else, nor to sell copies.

PRODUCING TAPES FOR SALE OR HIRE If you wish to sell or hire your own recordings, you need a Commercial Recording Licence from MCPS. (As well, of course, as all the relevant permissions.) The Copyright Act 1956 requires that you complete a statutory notice and pay certain royalties. MCPS will send you copies of these notice forms on request. You must give full details of all titles, the number you will be duplicating and the sale price (less VAT). Send the completed form back to MCPS and they will invoice you for the relevant amount. If you produce a repeat batch later, just let them know how many you are producing and they will invoice you again.

EDITING, DUBBING AND VOICE-OVERS The music industry does not like to have its products 'tampered with', by which they mean they do not like to have music edited, or to have anything added to it. This latter is called 'dubbing' and it includes anything added to the original recording, whether it is an additional instrument playing, sounds of animals or ocean waves, or a voice giving instructions to a horse rider. Unless of course, you have their permission and pay an appropriate royalty.

Even so, permission may not be forthcoming. Composers may not be prepared to let anyone interfere with their precious music at all, or they may just not like what you want to do. Record companies or publishers may have contracts giving exclusive rights on that piece of music. You can but ask.

The best way to do it (and this applies to getting all the permissions you need) is to track down the appropriate person, telephone them and talk over what you want to do, then write to confirm what was agreed. (Keep a copy!) If editing or dubbing is involved, ask if you may send them a rough copy tape of what you want to do, but do assure them that you will destroy any copies if permission is refused.

Summary

To allow the public performance of music, you need a licence from PRS. To play recorded music in public, you need licences from PRS and PPL. To copy recordings, you need permission of the copyright owners via a licence from MCPS. To edit or dub music, you need permission from the composer, lyricist and the publisher.

ENTERTAINMENTS LICENCES For public performances, you may also need an Entertainments Licence from your local council. This situation is very complex and subject to local laws as well as parliamentary change. Whether or not you do need a licence is dependent, for instance, on the exact location of your venue, whether it is a designated 'Indoor Sports Arena' and many other details. To be sure you are not breaking the law, check with your local licensing authority, via the Town Hall.

(The basic principles in this chapter apply all over the world, but local rules may differ in detail. Do check with your local rights societies.)

3

Choosing Music

Special Cassettes for Riders

You can buy cassettes of music specially made for riders. They are usually divided into sequences of walk, trot and canter, although some more sophisticated versions may contain a mixture, rather like a dressage test. The latter are more likely to have a commentary or schooling instructions, such as 'In trot, a 10m circle at B. On returning to the track . . .'

The musically aware may find the quality of some of these cassettes disappointing, and be particularly irritated by those where the music is played on a programmable electronic organ. These are the machines where one of a number of background beats is selected, and this beat continues until switched off. The musician then plays a tune on top of the beat, but this tune can often be drowned by the relentless background beat.

Which is not to say that all such tapes should be avoided, merely that you should be selective about what you buy. The producers of these tapes advertise regularly in the horse magazines, and they can be bought by mail order, or occasionally on trade stands at the bigger shows. However, do take the trouble to enquire if the necessary licences and permissions have been obtained, or you inadvertently infringe copyright by using the tapes, even if you do not do so in public.

Finding Your Own Music

No matter how good the special tapes may be, there are not that many of them available and the content will soon pall from constant repetition. You will then need to find some new music. Basically this means buying tapes and it is worth enlisting the help of your local record shop. The 'pop only' shops won't be much help, but a general shop should be staffed by people with a good knowledge of a wide spectrum of music. If you tell them what you want and why, and go in regularly, they will soon start suggesting pieces of music to you. These considerations also apply to record libraries, which are a cheap way of finding suitable pieces. This does not mean you should copy library records or tapes (copyright again) but that you can listen to a lot of music for a small fee instead of having to buy records that may not be suitable.

You might be able to record some music from the radio, but this is a pretty hit and miss method; for other than serious classical music, it is not listed in the programmes and you do not know when a suitable piece will be played. You could record a whole programme of short pieces of popular music, but there will be few pearls amongst a lot of unsuitable stuff. There will also be a lot of talking in between records. Your brain tunes a lot of this out when you have the radio on as background to other activities and you may not be aware of just how much chat there is until you hear it recorded. Nor do the average disc jockey's weak jokes bear repetition. And, of course, copyright infringement applies here too.

Where the radio is useful is that it brings pieces of music to your attention and it usually tells you what they are called and who is playing them. On the more serious programmes they even give you the name of the company that produced them and a record number. If you miss the title, or they don't give it (for instance if it is used in a play) write in and ask. State the date, time and title of the programme and tell them at what point in the programme the music was played. Don't forget to send a stamped addressed envelope. All this, of course, also applies to television.

What Sort of Music?

Obviously the type of music you select will be dependent on what you want it for, as well as your own personal taste. The only generalisation that can be made is that the rhythm must be appropriate to a horse's gaits, so very slow or very fast rhythms are out. Most authorities agree that modern waltzes are not suitable, but some concede that certain Viennese waltzes are usable.

One problem with these is that they tend to be too long for competitive purposes. *The Blue Danube* by Strauss, for instance, takes ten minutes. However, some have very long introductions (four and three-quarter minutes for *Wine, Women and Song*, also by Strauss) and the remainder might be a usable length. Another problem with Viennese waltzes is that they tend to start off very slowly and get faster as they go along. *The Blue Danube* is one of these.

An advantage is that they are divided up into a series of different tune sequences or variations, which offer opportunities for a change of rein or pattern. *The Blue Danube* has fourteen of these sequences, each 30 or 40 seconds long, and one, towards the end, of 20 seconds. The time length of the sequences is dependent on the speed at which it is played. In some pieces, this speed or tempo is constant, while in others it is varied. This may not be appropriate in dressage competitions unless extensions are called for.

Some of the other music of this period may also be useful-marches, polkas, galops and so on. If you have a taste for it, do try to get away from the more obvious pieces. If you or your friends visit Vienna there are plenty of records available of all sorts of obscure but charming pieces. Failing that, or a helpful assistant in your favourite record shop, try the Anglo-Austrian Society (see Useful Addresses).

BACKGROUND MUSIC Much of this sort of music, and most ballet music, comes under the heading of 'background' music. This means that while the general time, rhythm and beat should be appropriate to the gait, no attempt is made to match the horse's footfalls to the beats. For this reason, it is the best type of music for the novice competitor or the 'music for pleasure or schooling' situation.

Some classical music is also appropriate, the obvious example being Mozart. His light but mathematically precise music is a delight to ride to, but you would be wise to avoid using in public any of the pieces used by the Spanish Riding School if you do not want to be thought pretentious, or to invite comparisons with their standards of excellence.

A variation on pure classical music which might appeal are the 'pop' versions by such groups as Sky. Here the originals have been rhythmicised and performed on instruments which include the modern acoustic guitar. The opposite is popular and rock music played by symphony orchestras in the classical manner. These are wonderfully strong versions of pop 'standards'. One of the best series of these was called 'Rock Classics' by the London Symphony Orchestra, and it is not marred by the intrusive 'clapping machine' background used on some records.

POPULAR MUSIC 'Standards' are popular tunes which become part of musical history and are in continual demand by musicians and singers. These include many songs from the shows and musical films of the 1930s and 1940s and have more recently included many by the Beatles. Because of their strong tunes and tempos, many are suitable for riding. Listen to songs from South Pacific and consider the possibilities of flying changes to *I'm as corny as Kansas in August* or *I'm gonna wash that man right out of my hair*. Listen to all the Fred Astaire songs and think what you could do with *Putting on the Ritz* or *Top Hat, White Tie and Tails*. Peter Skellern recently did an album called *Skellern sings Astaire* with many of the better-known songs.

There are many popular piano players who have put together collections of standards, from the medleys of Charlie Kunz to Winifred Atwell or Bobby Crush and it is useful to note the different speeds at which they play. Bobby Crush gets through *The Entertainer* in two minutes and twenty seconds; Winifred Atwell in two minutes and forty seconds; while Joshua Rifkin (who was responsible for the recent revival of Scott Joplin's ragtime music) takes three minutes and fifteen seconds. We will return to this point later.

Most of the new tunes which become standards have first risen to the top of the hit parade listings, and if you want to be bang up to the minute in your choice, Radio One and the commercial radio stations are a fertile source of music. But do not just listen to the records at the top of the hit parade — there are many excellent tunes which hover in the lower levels of the charts. You are less likely to find other competitors using these than the top hits. Judges and spectators will soon get bored with the same tune, but they do like familiar music, where they know what comes next.

'NATIONAL' MUSIC This includes such areas as immediately recognisable instruments like bagpipes, and music where the style stamps its country of origin on it, like *Viva Espana*. This is a good area to look at when planning a quadrille or other costumed piece, but do take care to check the provenance of the tunes before you choose costumes or put different pieces together. It would not do, for instance, to provide blue cavalry uniforms for *The Battle Hymn of the Republic* (aka *John Brown's Body*) nor to tack *Marching Through Georgia* on to it! (It was the Yankees who marched through Georgia, burning towns and crops as they went.)

MUSIC FOR DIFFERENT GAITS It would be nice if one could say 'A march is always a walk, ragtime is always a trot' and so on, but it is not as simple as that, for there are tremendous variations in all types of music. For instance, one normally thinks of a polka as being a fast romp, but *Die Libelle* is so slow that you could do no more than walk to it. And anyway, are you sure you can recognise a polka, or a gavotte,

Some horses can't manage a polka

or a pavanne? What is far more reliable is your own recognition of the rhythm of footfalls in the different gaits. If you are not sure that the piece you like is right, get up on your horse and try to ride to it.

Using Video

If you have a video player and can get a tape of your horse working, you can use this to help in your selection of music. The video should consist of long periods of each level of each pace, and you play this on the television while you play various pieces of music against each gait until you get the right match.

Another way to check your recognition of gaits is to fix in your mind a particular piece of music which you know fits a particular gait. Then you just hum it to yourself to fix the rhythm in your head before you listen to a possible piece. The most difficult gait is canter, but there was a popular record a few years back about *The Day We Went to Bangor* which is just right.

Using a Metronome and Stopwatch

If you are really unsure of your ability to carry a rhythm in your head, or if you are dealing with a number of different horses, you will need an assistant with a stopwatch, and a metronome. One of you rides the horse, while the other counts strides per minute in each level of each gait and writes them down. (Don't forget each stride starts with a hind leg.)

Then you retire indoors and set the times on the metronome by moving the weight up or down the sweep (arm) to the appropriate mark. Then you start it and as the sweep reaches each side of its swing, it will click. Leave it running while you play the music and see how the clicks compare with the dominant beat in the bar.

For the non-technically inclined, it should be explained that music is divided into 'bars', which are further divided into 'beats'. If it goes BOOM boom boom boom, BOOM boom boom boom, it has four beats to the bar ('four time') and if it goes BOOM boom, BOOM boom, it has two beats to the bar ('two time'). It gets more complicated than that, but those are the essentials.

Four time is right for walk, two time for trot, but if the music is very fast, you might be able to use alternate beats for footfalls. The important thing is that each stride should start with the emphatic beat. It is nice if each beat involves a footfall — assuming that the rider has enough fine control over the horse to ensure that it does. With a novice rider or novice horse, it is wiser to avoid music with a strong beat, for this can only serve to emphasise unevenness in the gaits.

Speed of the Music

There are no hard and fast rules in music as to the precise speed at which a piece should be played. As was mentioned above, there can be considerable differences in tempo between performers, and in addition the tune may be 'arranged' to be played at vastly different speed than envisaged by the original composer.

Thus if you find that the piece you would like to use is not quite the right speed for your horse, you need not abandon it completely. Just keep looking for versions by different performers and timing them until you find one that is right. This will not be possible with brand new popular hits, for the performers in such cases will have protected their interests by denying others performing rights for a specified period.

What you should not try to do is alter the playing speed of records or cassettes, for this inevitably distorts the sound. If you have live musicians available to play for you, all you need do is demonstrate the tempo you want, either with the horse or with the metronome.

In most cases, minor adjustments of speed to suit the music will be within the scope of both horse and rider. Indeed, many horses will listen to the music and 'slot' themselves into the beat. This is an extension of the average human's inability to do anything other than march to a march.

CHANGES WITHIN THE GAITS This means that where the demands of a dressage test, or your inclination, call for a change in the level of the gait (e.g. from collected to extended

35

trot) you will need an appropriate change in the tempo of the music. While it is acceptable to change the piece of music for transitions to a different gait, it is not acceptable, either aesthetically or to avoid confusing the judge, to do so for changes of level. In such cases, your choice of music must be of a piece that has its own changes of tempo and/or tune sequence. The most obvious example of this is songs with verses and a chorus.

Suitable Music

Finally, but probably most importantly, the music you choose must suit the type and personality of the horse as well as his paces. Light tinkly pieces will suit a fine Thoroughbred, an Arab or a show pony, but they will not do for a Cob. The author had a chunky Thoroughbred cross Hanoverian, whose looks and personality were perfect for Souza's *Liberty Bell* (known to more people, perhaps, as the music from 'Monty Python's Flying Circus'). There was a show pony in the same yard whose paces were a perfect match for the *Steptoe* theme, but no-one ever suggested it other than as a threat when he was naughty.

Nor would the Steptoe theme be appropriate for the Best Trained Hack championship, any more than Christmas tunes would be in mid-summer. *Oh, what a beautiful morning* would be alright in spring or summer, provided you could guarantee it would not rain on the day and that you would not be called to perform after lunch.

One other consideration, especially valid for demonstration or display performances, is the possible attitudes of the audience. It really would not be tactful to play Yankee marching songs in the deep south of America or *The Red Flag* to a gathering of Conservatives. These are rather extreme examples, but you will get the general idea. Nor is it wise, if performing for an invited audience which you know will contain foreign dignitaries, to play music from their country. You may inadvertently choose something favoured by the opposing political faction, and even if not, they may consider this temerity rather than the politeness you intended.

4

Choreography

Basic Principles

In public situations, whether for display or competition, the object of the exercise is to produce something which is visually pleasing to the observers. This means that it should be symmetrical and easy to follow, which effectively means that the patterns should be fairly simple. Even in a dressage test, there is no need for the work on one rein to be a mirror image of the other, but even so, there should be some logical pattern.

The only way to be sure that you have the balance correct is to sit down and draw the movements. You will need a series of arena shapes — for illustrative purposes we will assume it to be a basic dressage arena, complete with markers. (Fig 1) To get the idea, start off by drawing the movements of a standard dressage test, using different colours or different marks to show the gaits. Figs 2 to 5 show the Preliminary test No 4.

Designing a Dressage Test

Once you have done that, you can think of composing your own patterns. Let us consider a Novice Freestyle test, where the compulsory movements are 15 m circles in working trot, left and right; 20 m circles in working canter, left and right; lengthened strides in trot; medium walk; free walk; and two halts which must be at the beginning and end of the test. The test must take four minutes, and you may add any movements of your own to make up the time, providing they are those normally required at Novice level. (This rule applies at all levels.)

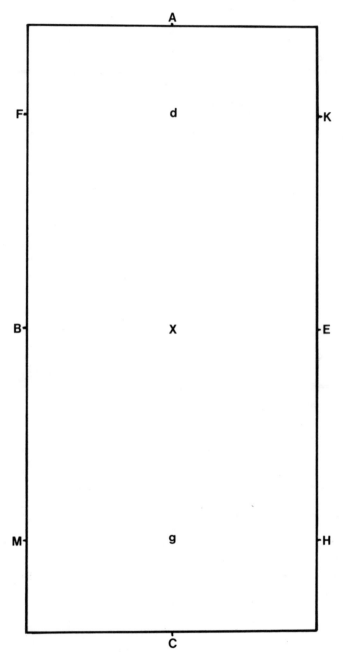

Figure 1 Standard dressage arena

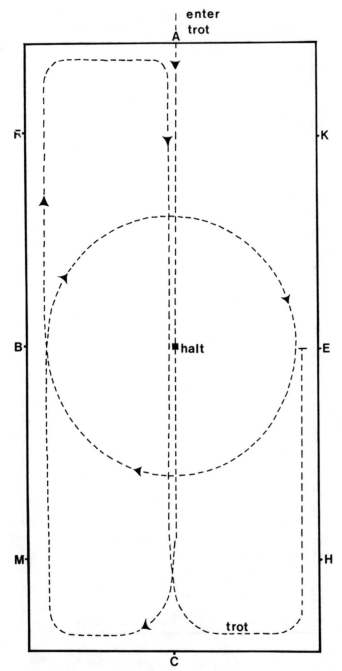

Figure 2 Preliminary test No. 4, Part 1

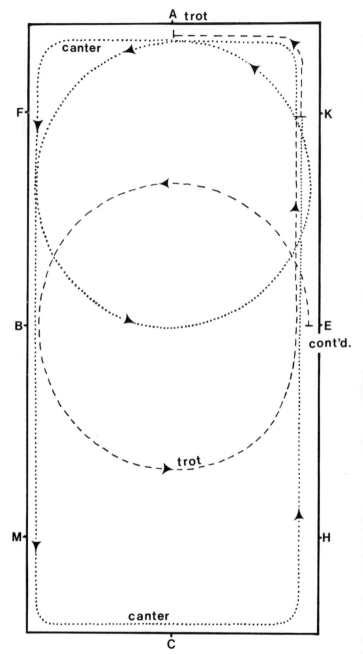

Figure 3 (continued from Figure 2)   Preliminary test No. 4, Part 2

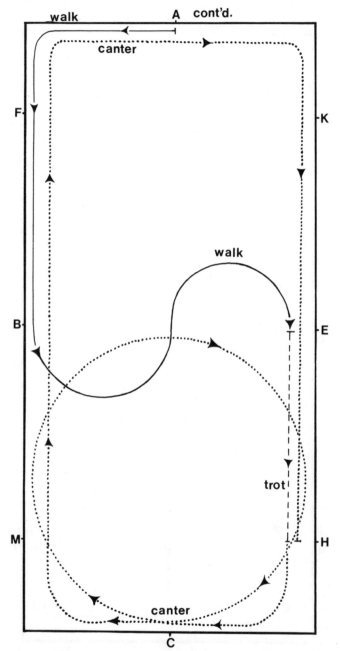

Figure 4 (continued from Figure 3) Preliminary test No. 4, Part 3

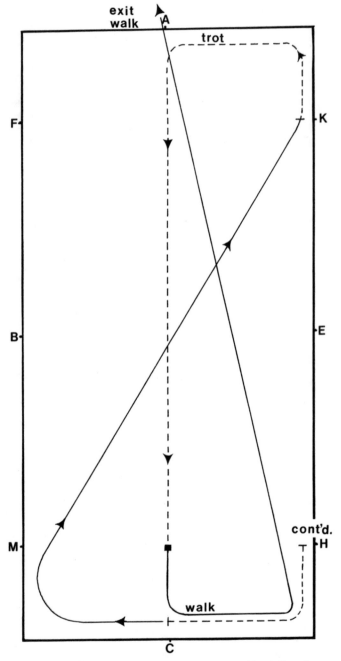

Figure 5 (continued from Figure 4)   Preliminary test No. 4, Part 4

Figs 6 to 9 show a possible pattern for this test.
A Enter working trot;
X Halt, salute
Proceed working trot;
C Track right
B 15 m circle right;
B A K working trot;
K X M change the rein and show some lengthened strides;
M Working trot;
E 15 m circle left
A Working canter left;
B 20 m circle left;
H X F change the rein;
at X Working trot;
A Working canter right;
E 20 m circle right;
E C B F Working canter;
F Working trot;
A Medium walk;
K X M Change the rein, Free walk on a long rein;
M Medium walk;
C Working trot;
H X F Change the rein and show some lengthened strides;
F Working trot;
A Down centre line;
G (or when the bell rings) Halt salute.

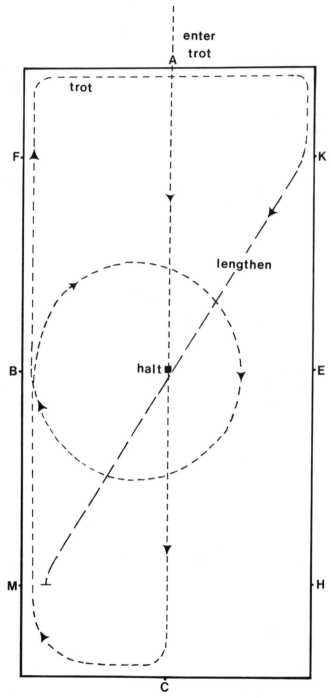

Figure 6 Sample Novice freestyle test, Part 1

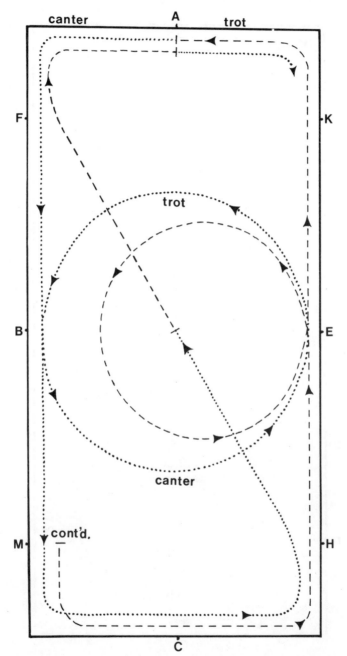

Figure 7 (continued from Figure 6)   Sample Novice freestyle test, Part 2

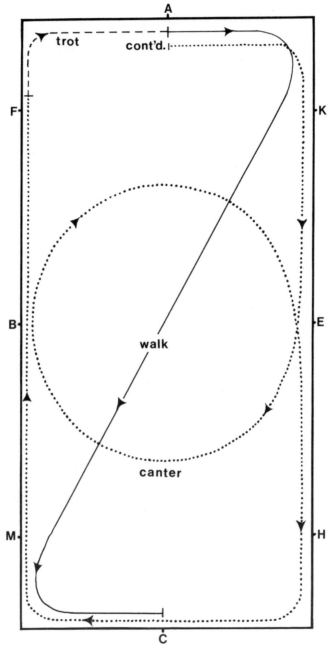

Figure 8 (continued from Figure 7)   Sample Novice freestyle test, Part 3

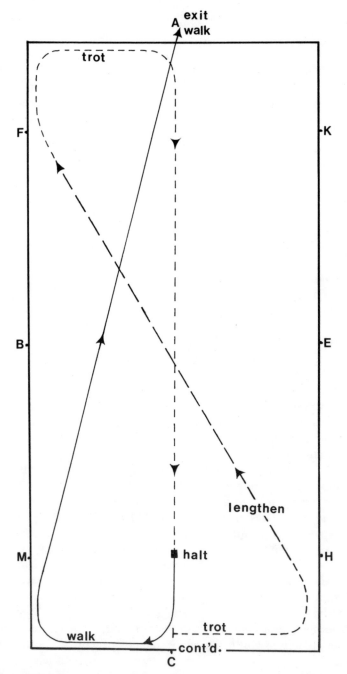

Figure 9 (continued from Figure 8)   Sample Novice freestyle test, Part 4

TIMING At this point, you have to ride through your pattern while somebody times it. Part of your early work with the stopwatch should include not only how many strides per minute your horse takes in each gait, but also how long it takes to perform each basic movement. This will have given you an approximate idea of timing, but where dressage tests are concerned, you must be accurate in your use of time. The tests are timed from the move-off from the entrance halt to the final halt.

Once you know how long your pattern takes to ride through, and how long individual movements take, you can then work out what to add to or subtract from your pattern. However, for the sake of ease of fitting music to the pattern, as well as ease of remembering it when you go in to compete, it is wise to keep all the work in each gait together. Obviously there are unavoidable exceptions to this, such as the necessity to trot between walk and canter, and changes of rein, but the design of your pattern should keep it to a minimum.

ADDITIONAL CONSIDERATIONS FOR DRESSAGE Although we have referred above to movements commencing from dressage letter markers, this was for illustrative purposes. For tests, you do not have to use the markers and can ignore them if you wish. However, newcomers to these competitions may feel more confident of the accuracy of their movements if they do use the markers. You will not be penalised if you do use them. Whichever, you should use the whole arena, and when performing a test where the compulsory movements fall far short of the time requirements, your additional movements should be roughly equal on both reins.

There is no reason why you should not apply the general principles of ringcraft in a dressage competition, and that is to show yourself to the best advantage. One of the main ways of doing this is to perform your advanced movements coming towards the judge, so you will need to design your test so that the simpler movements take you to the far end of the arena to start the more advanced movements.

Another major consideration, especially for novice riders or horses, is where you locate your changes of gait. If you are at

Perform your advanced movements coming towards the judge

all uncertain about your ability to produce accurately located transitions, it is wise to make them on circles, where delay is less obvious. Do not forget that different surfaces may affect your gait timings and that uneven patches (most likely to be encountered at small shows on grass) could affect your rhythm.

Do design your test in such a way that the judge can be sure you have performed all the movements. This may sound silly, but it is possible, for instance, to mistake an inadequate trot extension across the arena as a mere change of rein, executed rather hurriedly!

Finally, do be certain that you are working from an up-to-date version of the test requirements.

Non-Competitive Choreography _____

Here the task is much simpler, and done the other way round, in that you start with the music and fit your pattern to it. Nor do you have the restraints of working to a specified time or compulsory movements.

The only time restraints involved are those of finding a piece, or putting together a piece, long enough to show what you want, but short enough to avoid boring your audience. The more horses involved, the longer you can get away with, but unless you are acting out a complex story with dialogue and new characters coming in, eight minutes is the absolute maximum, and six is better.

As a point of interest, the average popular tune lasts two and a half minutes and if all you have to show is basic gaits, that is quite enough for each individual rider. For displays, you are further restricted to trot and canter, and maybe an extended canter at the end, for walk is too slow and your audience's attention will soon wander.

If you have good advanced gaits to show (and you leave yourself open to scornful criticism if they are not good) you can go on longer. The Grand Prix Freestyle test is six minutes and there is plenty for even the uneducated to watch in that. The best advanced displays are usually those where the difficulty of the movements builds as the display progresses, leaving the pirouettes and sequence changes to the end.

Once you have mapped out the piece of music, you can consider patterns. As before, you should consider symmetry, but it should be done with the position of the audience in mind. For a dressage test you must aim your movements at the judge, but a display might have the audience all round at a big show, or at one end or side of an indoor school.

If you are designing a piece for a specific display, you can take the location of the audience (or the most important bit of it, for instance the Royal Box) into account. If your piece is to travel round several locations it is best to design it with all the interesting bits in the middle of the arena. Wherever it is, you should never disappear into corners and particularly not to do twiddly bits. On the other hand, if your horse is prone

to bloody mindedness, such corners might be useful for a
rapid discussion on discipline!

TIMING   The preliminary work remains the same, timing the
gaits and various movements. The next task is to dissect your
chosen piece of music with a stopwatch and notepad. Time
each section of the music and note which gait it will suit. It is
advisable to do this in private, or with head-phones, for you
will have to keep starting and stopping the music, and playing
the same piece over and over again.

ADJUSTING MOVEMENTS TO FIT THE MUSIC   You can,
as discussed in Chapter 1, edit your music so that each section
is a precise length. If you do not have the facilities or the
inclination to do this, you will have to adjust your movements.

Say you want to do a figure of eight (two circles joining) in
canter and the music is divided neatly into two bits — but one
bit is two seconds longer than the other. When you consider
that the average horse can canter all round a 20 × 40 m arena in
30 seconds, you realise how long two seconds is. You can't
adjust the speed of canter much or you will lose the beat, but
you can make one circle a little larger, or delay your strike off.

You can go right into corners one end and not the other, or
you can make your figure of eight the show version (two half
circles joined by straight lines) which allows quite a bit of
juggling. There are plenty of such adjustments that you can
make, but what is immediately obvious to the audience is dis-
torted shapes, such as square or oblong circles or wavering lines.

The whole thing about these adjustments is that you can
only do them if you know your music by heart. You must
know while you listen to each bar, what the next bar is, and
when there is a change of tune or tempo. Then, and only then,
do you know how long you have before you must be at a
specific place to do something different.

Choreography for Side-Saddle

Assuming that the horse is well schooled and well balanced;
that the saddle is properly balanced and fitted to the horse;
and that the rider is competent enough to sit square and straight

at all times; then there is no need to make any concessions to side-saddle when choreographing. If any of the above do not pertain, then special consideration must be given to the work on the left rein.

Tight left turns and small circles should be avoided, as they will only serve to encourage the rider to drop her weight back to the left. Not only does this unbalance the horse, it also causes ugly distortion in the rider as she strives to regain her equilibrium, and it also impedes her ability to apply the aids. The faster the gait, the worse the problem; and if the footing is poor, the greater the risk of the imbalance bring the horse down.

The commonest fault in a side-saddle rider is this tendency to drop the left hip back. This is frequently the fault of the saddle as much as the rider, but wherever the blame lies, the result is the same — the horse moves his quarters away from the extra weight on the left. On left-handed circles and corners, he will swing his quarters out, and in what should be straight lines, he will proceed on two tracks with his quarters to the right. With this in mind, if planning straight lines either directly to or away from the audience, it is wise to start them from a right turn, when the rider has more chance of at least starting straight.

Another common problem with novice side-saddle riders is the transition to canter. This is not just confined to the left rein, where the problem is usually a nervous rider applying the brakes, but also to the right rein where the problem is of a dropped left hip and consequent maladjustment of shoulders and hands causing a left bend. Whichever pertains, such novices will always find it easier if the transition to canter is on an already established circle.

In a perfect world one would not need to apply such considerations. But it is always tempting to include side-saddles in quadrilles and displays, even if horses and riders are not experienced with them. In such situations, the value of their visual impact should be balanced against the riders' safety and the risk of making the horses' back sore.

(Choreography for pairs and teams is dealt with in Chapter 6.)

5

Competitions

Dressage

There are Freestyle to Music classes available at all levels, from riding club to national championship shows. There are also special sponsored Freestyle to Music championships, with qualifying classes at affiliated shows.

All these tests are judged on the basis of 50 per cent of the marks for 'technical performance' in the compulsory movements and 50 per cent for 'artistic merit'. Of those artistic marks, half are for gaits – freedom, regularity, impulsion, submission, lightness and ease of the movements. The other half are for the composition of the test, choreography and incorporation of the music. As always, with the technical part, the quickest way to lose marks is to ride inaccurate figures, so be sure circles are circular, straight lines straight and halts straight and square.

Both sections are judged by the same judge, but at some championship finals there may be an additional prize for best artistic impression which is awarded by a separate judge. In ordinary tests, if two riders have the same overall total, the higher place will be awarded to whichever has the higher marks for artistic impression.

The compulsory movements obviously vary with the level of test, but they all require the normal halt-salute at the beginning and end of the test. The timing runs from the move-off from the beginning halt to the final halt. At all levels, although certain movements are compulsory, the order in which they are performed and the place in the arena where they are performed is optional.

In all other respects, the normal dressage rules and conventions apply.

CHANGING ROUTINES There is no requirement for either your pattern or music to be original at each show and you could spend the rest of your competitive life using one routine for each level. This assumes that you don't mind hearing people say 'Oh Lord, she's doing her *Sting* routine again!' You do not even need to produce a new routine or music for the finals of a championship, although most of those who qualify do tend to, in the interests of polishing their performance.

What is not advisable, particularly if your horse tends to anticipate, is to make last minute changes of pattern without changing the music, or you may have unseemly arguments about where you should be going and in what gait.

There is no requirement for routines to be designed solely by the rider, so there is no reason why you should not have someone to help you with music and choreography. There are several people who will do this for a fee. Some want to see the horse work in the flesh, others will do it from a video.

CHOICE OF MUSIC There are a few additional considerations to those discussed in Chapter 3 when choosing and editing music for dressage tests.

The main consideration is that the music is meant to enhance the horse's performance, not dominate it. For this reason it is wise to avoid music with a very strong beat, as this can only serve to emphasise any loss of rhythm, especially in trot.

Another thing to avoid is music that is a little too fast for your horse's natural gaits. If you are nervous you will tend to hurry anyway and you will end up scurrying through your test, making silly mistakes and making the judge feel out of breath. If you are inclined towards this sort of nervousness, choose music that is a little slow, and let it help calm you down.

In view of the dressage world's general conviction that you cannot ride to waltzes, you should avoid them unless you happen to know that a particular judge does not share the conviction. Some judges also dislike music with songs, as they find the vocal distracting. Vocals also tend to dominate, and may prevent you editing as you would wish, for you must not cut the song anywhere except at the end of a verse or chorus.

The whole area of which judges like what sort of music might be worth some thought. Whilst judges should not be influenced by their own taste, they are only human. If a judge has a violent dislike for, say, pop music, he will not particularly appreciate any form of choreography to it.

How you find out any particular judge's taste in music is another matter, unless you are prepared to complete tables of winning and losing music throughout the season and match it to judges. But beware — this may not be considered sporting!

Judges may be influenced by your taste in music

Even if you do not do it for this reason, it is a good idea to make a note of what music is being used. On the positive side, you may hear a piece that you feel you could use to advantage or that will set your mind off on a new track. On the negative side, you will hear certain pieces so often that you will realise you must not use them — *The Sting* and *In the Mood* for instance, are used by so many people that they have become cliches.

Reproducing Music for tests

You must take your music to shows on one cassette. The organisers will provide the player, and a 'technician' to play the cassette, but you are allowed to have your own 'expert' to advise the technician while you are performing.

The British Horse Society (BHS) suggests that you should fade down the music for transitions, and this is not a bad idea, except that it does make it obvious if your timing is out. They also suggest use of the 'Pause' button when changing music for a change of gait, but this also commits you to that transition and may not be aesthetically acceptable. If you are not sure of your ability to produce precision, it is better to use background type music and have transitions on circles.

Your music may start as you move off from your halt, or before you enter the arena, and should stop with your final halt. On the whole, unless you have chosen an innocuous piece of background music, it is better if it starts with the move-off.

Once you have your piece of music as you want it, add a 'lead in', which can be an announcement of your horse's name and your own, or a count down from 5 to 1. When you are in the arena, you cannot see the button being pressed and you could be caught unawares. Then make several copies of it to circumvent Murphy's Law and take two copies to the show.

Be sure your cassettes are labelled clearly with your name, the horse's name and details of the class. Leave room on the label to add your number when you get to the show. If you are competing on more than one horse, or in more than one class, each piece of music should be on a separate cassette, all carefully labelled. The tape should be rewound to the start of the music, so all the technician has to do is press the 'Play' button. If you are not providing an expert to advise the technician, clear instructions should be written on the cassette box (e.g. 'This tape is ready to commence when PLAY is pressed. Please press PLAY as soon as I have entered and halted. There is a 5 4 3 2 1 countdown at the beginning.').

Licences

The BHS holds a PRS licence which covers all affiliated dressage shows. They do not have any licences from, or arrangements with, PPL, or MCPS. If these are required, you must obtain them yourself.

Riding clubs are not covered by the BHS's PRS licence. Riding club and other unaffiliated shows may not hold a PRS or any other licence, and you should find out before competing whether you need to obtain your own licences. All these shows constitute public performances.

Side-Saddle

The Side-Saddle Association holds Freestyle to Music classes — one adult and one junior — at its annual National Show. There are also classes at some area shows. They count as non-affiliated classes, with low prize money, but do have prizes in kind as well.

The classes are run in the same way as dressage tests, in a 20 × 40 m area, with the marks awarded 50 per cent for technical accuracy and 50 per cent for artistic interpretation. The time is three and a half minutes and you must show walk, trot and canter on both reins.

You do not have to be a member of the SSA to compete, but you must ride side-saddle. Although you will not be judged on your turnout, you will be expected to dress as for a side-saddle equitation class — sober coloured habit, collar and tie, with hunting cap for juniors and bowler and veil for adults. You may carry a whip no more than 1 m in length.

You should produce your music on a cassette. Like the BHS, the SSA has a PRS licence, but no others. These shows constitute a public performance, so you should ensure you are properly licenced.

Best Trained Hack

This class is held at the British Show Hack, Cob and Riding Horse Association's National Championship Show. To qualify, the horse must have been placed first, second or third in any affiliated show class during that season, and be registered with the Association.

There is no specified size of arena, but the show must not exceed three minutes. At the time of writing, the content of the show is under discussion, but the 1986 rules stated that it must include rein-back, and move forward from either rein-back or halt into trot or canter. Judges were looking for style, smooth transitions, collection and extension, and some work with the reins in one hand. Obedience to the leg, defined as 'half-pass at the walk, turn on the haunches and flying change in a straight line' if correctly executed, would gain extra marks.

Exhibits may be ridden side-saddle or astride, but must be in double bridle or pelham. Obvious resistances such as being overbent or behind the bit are penalised.

Riders may take their own cassettes (and arrange their own licences, as the Association has none) or the show organisers will provide light background music.

Riding Clubs Quadrille

This competition is held every year, with a qualifying class which is held at Stoneleigh. The four highest marked teams go forward to the championship at the Horse of the Year Show.

The competition is open to teams of four horses and riders from affiliated riding clubs. The riders must be full members of the BHS as well as the riding club and must be over 17 years of age. No more than one rider may have been placed first, second or third in an international dressage competition. The horses do not have to belong to the riders, but must belong to members of the club, to the club itself, or a riding school normally used by the club.

The quadrille must take no more than five minutes (and not much less!) timing being from the opening form-up and salute to the final salute. The arena will be 23 m × 55 m and will have centre, quarter and corner markers. No jumps or cavaletti may be used and props, animals or people other than the actual team are not allowed. The judges are located halfway down the right-hand side from the entrance.

A full copy of the rules should be obtained (from the BHS Riding Clubs Office. See Useful Addresses). A typed script of about 100 words, describing the quadrille must be sent to this office two weeks before the qualifying show, for distribution to the judges and commentator.

The object of the exercise is to produce a display of horsemanship to music, which will delight the eye. It may be a pure dressage display, or a narrative display, but the emphasis should be on horsemanship and teamwork rather than pure theatre. It does not have to use pure dressage movements.

All four riders must take an active part, but their movements do not have to be mirror images of all four, or even two pairs. Any of them may engage in movements not done by the others. For instance, Three Little Maids From School (St Trinians style) each playing in a corner until the school marm (in gown and mortarboard) arrives to call them to order for their minuet lesson.

Of the 120 possible marks, 25 are for content of programme — the choice and pattern of the movements and the skill and ingenuity with which they are linked — and 25 for performance — the ability of the horses to carry out the movements and the quality of their gaits and also the standard of riding. Artistic impression carries 50 marks — the quadrille as a display of horsemanship and as entertainment, and the suitability and use of the music.

The final 20 marks are for appearance. This is judged by a rigorous inspection before the display, usually in the collecting ring. Judges look at the condition and turnout of the horses, and while they do not necessarily expect them to be matched in colour, they do expect them to match in other respects. All tails should be the same length and plaited or pulled in the same manner. All manes should be identical in length and thickness, and if plaited, should have the same number of plaits. Leg bandages should be sewn in and identical.

Substances used to mark coats which could be irritants are not appreciated, nor is greasepaint on the face which could run into the eyes.

The tack should also be identical, although the judges are not so fussy about bits as they used to be. The tack must be safe — if your storyline calls for silken reins, then it must be silk-covered leather, not just silk. There is no bar to side-saddles.

The riders may wear modern or period costume, but this will also be subjected to detailed scrutiny. Although the judges will not ask you to unbutton jackets to look at linings, they may well turn up coat tails or skirts for that purpose. They will expect period or military costumes to be authentic throughout — footwear, hats, wigs and gloves should be correct for the rest of the costume.

Some of the narrative displays in recent years have involved Beefeaters, Toy Soldiers, Clowns and a Square Dance. It becomes more and more difficult each year to think up original themes, but sources of inspiration could include popular films or stage shows; fairy stories or other myths or legends. The childrens' section of your local library is well supplied with the latter.

Obviously the music must suit the story, but one thing to keep in mind is that the audience at the Horse of the Year Show plays a large part in selecting the winners, so do not choose music that may be too esoteric for that audience.

For the qualifying show, you must produce your music on a cassette, and all the usual licences must be obtained. The BHS Riding Clubs office holds no licences for this purpose, nor does the average riding club as a matter of course.

The music at the Horse of the Year Show will be played by the band and this is covered by the Show's PRS licence. You will not be able to rehearse with the band, so you must use your tape. You will be allowed a set time for this rehearsal which will allow you to run through your whole routine two or three times.

Do not forget that all horses will need a valid inoculation certificate for the final, and also possibly for the qualifying show.

It would be wise to ascertain, before you get too involved, what proportion, if any, of the costs will be borne by your riding club and what will happen to any prizes.

6

Teamwork

A team, in this context, means more than one horse/rider combination, and covers *pas des deux* (two) quadrille (four) or any other number. Apart from complications of choreography, there is no reason why a team should not be odd-numbered, but even numbers are usual.

Whilst a pair of riders may manage to plan, choreograph and practise on their own, any larger number requires a team coach, who remains on the ground throughout. This chapter is principally aimed at that coach.

Choosing Your Team

However many people are to be members of your team, your priority must be to ensure that they all understand and accept the time commitment. You cannot put together and polish a performance in a few days and everyone must be prepared to devote more than one day a week for several weeks, or even months, to the project. For this reason, you should avoid students with exams looming or young people who want to spend time in pursuit of the opposite sex. Given a choice of season, spring is the best time to start, for then there will be less likelihood of 'flu or hunting injuries disrupting rehearsals.

You should ideally have a spare horse and rider ready as stand-ins in case anyone drops out or goes sick at a critical moment. They should be actively involved in rehearsals, and if all parts are not identical, should be familiar with all of them so they can be slotted in where necessary.

Horses should be the same size and type

Assuming that you are performing a symmetrical display, rather than a 'ballet', the horses should all be the same size and of the same breed or type. Their action should be the same — one knee-lifter in a team of daisy-cutters spoils the whole effect. They should all be at the same stage of schooling, or you will have to level the best down to the worst, or spend too much of your time coaching individual members of the team. If you have a choice, consider also the horses natural 'handedness' and bend preference.

Whilst all the horses do not have to be exactly the same colour, they should more or less match in pairs or be good foils for each other. (In a perfect world, all leg and face markings would be identical, or mirror in pairs.) The owners must be prepared to allow identical mane and tail plaiting and trimming, and if performing in winter, all clips must be the same.

Mixtures of mares and geldings may create problems, especially in summer. Using stallions is dependent on their willingness to keep their mind on the music (and your willingness to see small children point and say 'Ooh Mummy — what's THAT?').

You do not need kickers under any circumstances. Choreography is complicated enough without having to keep one horse's back end away from the others all the time.

The riders should be of similar physique, allowing of course, for the inherent size differences between male and female. They should all be of equal intelligence — there are few things as infuriating for all concerned as one dumbo who can't learn the pattern. For perfection, they should all be either left- or right-handed. You may not think this is relevant, but it can make a difference to the execution of shapes and movements such as crossovers where fine judgement of line is needed.

The ability to judge speed and distance is important, especially closing distances in situations where riders are coming at each other from opposite sides to meet or pass at a central point. If your riders cannot do this accurately, you should avoid such movements rather than perform them badly.

This ability is part of the spatial location skill of proprioception and it is tied in with co-ordination. A drill instructor will test for this ability by seeing if recruits can march laterally (i.e. swinging the right hand and right leg forward together); starting with thumb on trouser seam, then pointing to where the foot will fall, then a free swing. If in doubt about the members of your team, you might try this exercise. Don't forget, it is the one who gets things wrong who stands out!

'Dressing' and Synchronisation

Dressing is a military term meaning, in this context, alignment with a point. Thus two people riding in a dressage arena are in alignment when one is at B and the other at E, or K and M, the point being X. If they have come down the centre line to A, turned in opposite directions and have not arrived at B and E

simultaneously, they are out of alignment and their dressing is incorrect. They should, having parted, have kept an eye on each other and adjusted their speed to keep their dressing. Several pairs of riders performing the same movement should each reach B and E together and M and H together. Similarly, if four riders are on a circle, they should all be an exact quarter circle away from each other all the way round.

This is one of the most important skills in team riders. They must keep an eye all the time on the others and adjust their gaits or length of stride to keep their dressing correct. In some situations this may mean riding a slightly smaller circle than their partner, or turning a little short for a corner. If it is an ongoing problem of different striding horses, you must plan for it when designing patterns, to ensure the shorter striding horse is always on the inside.

Synchronisation of stride is also important in any situation where riders are in line abreast. Lack of synchronisation is very obvious when a pair or the team are performing straight lines in trot. To an observer on the sidelines, the horses' legs twinkle, when there should only seem to be one set of legs, all moving together; and the riders' heads bob up and down at different times, instead of all together. The head bobbing is also apparent to centre line observers; and, from behind, the horses' quarters seem to undulate at random.

The answer to this is rising trot with all riders on the same diagonal and all rising together. If your team consists of riders incapable of achieving this simple synchronisation, then your choreography must keep them apart.

Problems

The main problems arising in team situations, assuming equal ability of all horses and riders, come from horses who take a strong liking or disliking to other horses. Dislike usually manifests itself as a reluctance to stay or pass close alongside, but in extreme cases it can involve attempts to bite or kick. The only cure is to keep these horses well separated, or dispense with the aggressor altogether.

More likely, and potentially more embarrassing, is the horse who wants to stay with his friend and won't turn left if the friend is turning right. This requires anticipation and firmness from the rider, but it might be wise to avoid stable mates in the team.

As a general point, it is not good idea to change the position of any horse in the team once the patterns have been decided. Horses have excellent memories and most of them learn their part and the music quickly. A horse who has learnt to turn left when the music goes 'tiddley pom pom pom' is likely to argue if his rider asks him to turn right or go straight on.

If you get continual nonsenses when all the riders come together at any point, it is useful to use a video. Not only does it allow you to pinpoint a particular culprit (and the more of them there are, the more likely they are to say 'Not me!') it also lets them see what is going on and how to correct it.

If it is your intention to use side-saddles at the finished performance, they should be used all the way through practises. Although a competent side-saddle rider should be able to perform all the movements, there are differences in balance and distancing potentials. For the inexperienced side-saddle rider or horse, the differences are magnified. In either case, it is stupid to introduce this sort of variable at the last minute.

Although not strictly speaking a problem, one point that does require careful thought is where to locate transitions. As with everything else, this depends on the ability of the riders and the obedience of the horses, but unless each rider has precise control, transitions should be done when the riders are separated. This way, it is not so obvious if one horse is two strides behind the others and the greater the separation, the less likely the observer's eye to be on more than one horse.

Team Choreography

Before you do anything else, there is one basic decision you must make, and having done so, you must stick to it for the rest of your career as a team coach. When two riders meet face to face, which side do they pass — right shoulder to right shoulder, or left to left? For most of us, this decision has already been made by convention, but there are many riders who have never ridden in a formal manege situation and do not realise the convention exists. Even they will soon realise the confusion that can arise if the rule is not made and stuck to.

Incidentally, whatever your local convention, if you intend to use side-saddles at any time, do remember that the rider's legs are on the left and her whip is on the right. While closer passes can be made right to right, whips should be kept close to the horse's side during that pass.

This potential whip problem also occurs when one of a pair rides side-saddle. The convention is for the astride rider, originally a man of course, to ride on the lady's right and thus have his right hand (and sword) available to protect her. If the man is too close (and in historical costume do remember that this extreme closeness would only be proper if he were her husband or brother) his horse may object to her whip. The other snag about his being on the right is that it prevents her from making the easier right turns if they want to go their separate ways.

This brings up the point of whether all riders should ride on both reins. In the Riding Clubs Quadrille they ought to, but in other situations it may not be necessary. If it is essential, at some point the riders are going to have to change sides and it is easier to do this once only, at half-time, rather than keep jockeying for position. The easiest way to do it is to bring everyone into single file then form off into pairs or whatever the other way round.

DRAWING PATTERNS Once you have made these fundamental decisions, and done the basic work of timing your music and horses, it is literally 'back to the drawing board' to plan patterns. At this stage you should stay fairly fluid in your ideas, for what looks good on paper may not work properly on the ground. The best way is to decide which set movements you want to perform, ride each through a few times to see which horses should be in which positions, and then see how to connect the movements together. The more riders you have, the more difficult this is, so the rule should be 'more means simpler'.

Resist the urge to do a series of complex moves, for often what you think is terribly clever only confuses the audience. Resist also the urge to juggle individual horses around too much, for unless horses and riders are all perfectly matched, this will be obvious to observers and they are bound to wonder why. By all means reverse the positions of 1 and 2 *and* 3 and 4, but don't move 1 to 2 in one movement, then to 3 in the next unless they all move round one place.

Once you have your patterns worked out in their final form, make a copy of the whole thing for each rider, with their part marked clearly in a different colour or highlighter. Make it clear that each is expected to know her part by the next rehearsal and give each a copy of the music so she can learn that too.

It often helps if the next rehearsal is without horses. Mark out a scaled down arena, allow each rider to carry her chart, play the music and go through it on foot. Do a bit at a time, then run right through until everybody is sure where they have to go. It might be tactful to make this a private rehearsal — it is embarrassing enough playing gee-gees without an audience!

Whether performed on one track or two, as a general principle the simplest movements are those which separate the members of the team and keep them apart. Although they have to watch their dressing, they do not have to worry quite so much about matching a partner's steps. These are often the most satisfactory visually, too, as long as the individual patterns are mirrored. You could actually produce a perfectly satisfactory display for a non-horsey audience by bringing your team in to the centre, then separating it and keeping each rider circling on her own and occasionally changing corners.

Equally, for a very knowledgeable audience, you could base a whole display on keeping your team in line abreast throughout. If they did no more than figures of eight and a wheel, they would need to be highly skilled to maintain their dressing all the time. If you feel like trying it, consider the possibilities of adding a bar or ribbon which all must hold, or pennants on poles or lances.

For most purposes, however, you will want a balanced mix of movements that involve the riders separating and coming back together for a while before separating again.

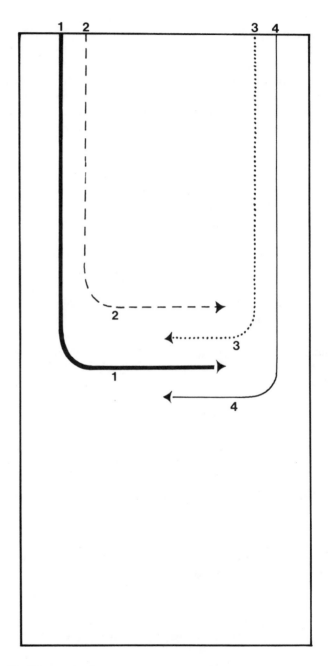

Figure 10 Countermarch

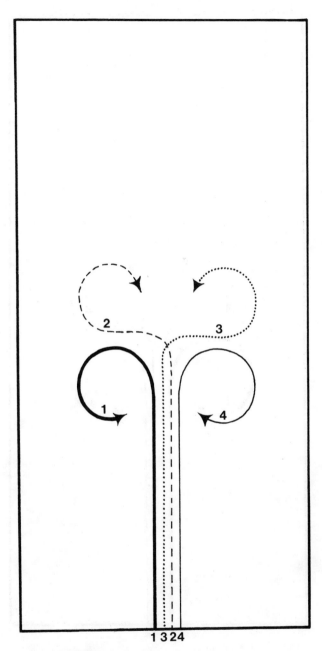

Figure 11 Cloverleaf, Method 1

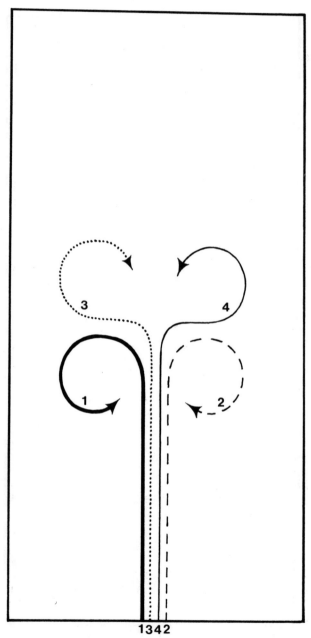

1342

Figure 12 Cloverleaf, Method 2

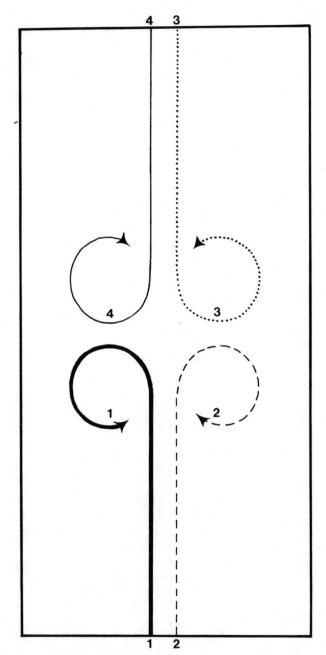

Figure 13 Cloverleaf, Method 3

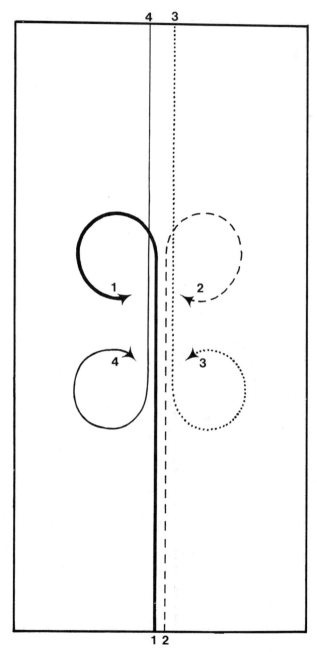

Figure 14 Cloverleaf, Method 4

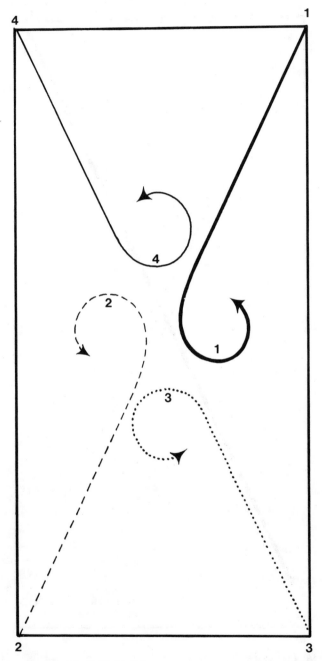

Figure 15 Cloverleaf, Method 5

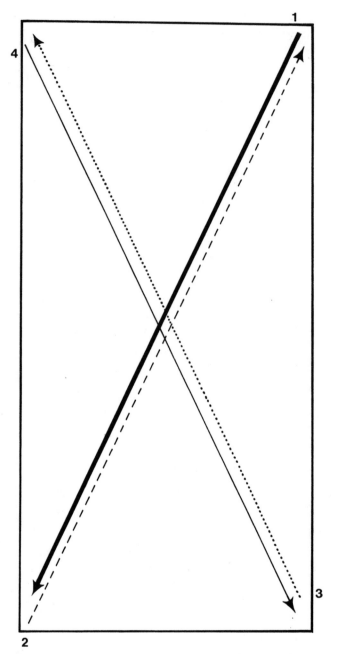

Figure 16 Crossover

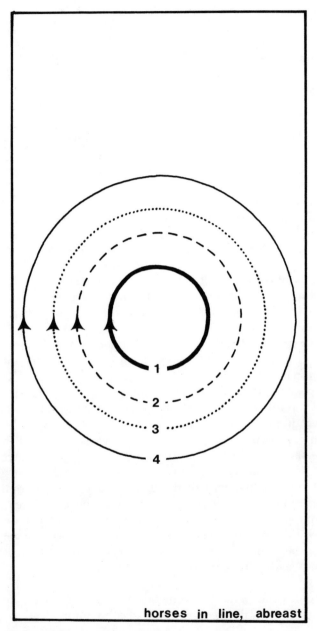

Figure 17 Wheel (horses in line abreast)

The Standard Movements _____

(For illustrative purposes it is assumed that the team consists of four horses.)

COUNTERMARCH This involves two pairs of riders approaching each other from opposite directions. Each pair should be far enough apart to allow one of the other pair to pass between them. Unless using lateral movements to separate each pair as they approach the centre point, it is best if they stagger their turn into the passing line so as to ride straight across with no obvious deviation. See Fig 10. (This movement is much more impressive with large teams, and is popular with military or police display teams.)

CLOVERLEAF There are several variations on this theme, but all involve each rider performing a small circle in her corner of the centre of the arena. It can be started by two pairs coming up the centre line and either — Fig 11 — the leading pair (1 and 2) turning left then splitting to turn left and right while the hind pair (3 and 4) does the opposite, or — Fig 12 — the two left riders (1 and 3) turning left then splitting left and right, while the right riders (2 and 4) turn right and split. Alternatively — Fig 13 — the two pairs can approach from opposite sides and split before they meet or — Fig 14 — after. All these risk the potentially embarrassing problem of horses who do not want to part. To avoid this — Fig 15 — all riders can approach from opposite corners, each peeling off to circle the same way just before the centre point. (It is always easier to converge than diverge.)

From the first four of these, you then have the options of performing one full circle and carrying on as before, or performing one and a bit circles to form different pairs or send each rider off on her own. The fifth is not so easy to get out of in a single circle without a crossover, but one and a half circles sends each rider back the way she came.

CROSSOVER This movement, if performed at anything other than walk, requires split second timing and is potentially dangerous. The faster it is done, the more difficult and dangerous it is, for the more the risk of a collision. It should not be performed without due consideration of the hazards.

Each rider approaches the centre point from her own corner with the intention of passing the other riders by as slim a margin as possible. See Fig 16. 1 crosses first, then 2, then 3, then 4. The trick is for each to leave her corner one or two strides later than her predecessor. If you repeat this movement, it is actually easier the next time, as the riders are already staggered.

WHEEL Here the riders perform concentric circles while keeping in line abreast — Fig 17. The inside horse must take small slow steps, the outside horse fast long ones, which usually means walk for 1, slow trot for 2, fast trot for 3 and canter for 4. You can start and finish it in line abreast, which involves some tricky transition timing or with each rider approaching from a different corner, adjusting her speed as necessary to get in line. (If you have eight in the team, you can also countermarch within the wheel.)

PEELOFFS/CONJUNCTIONS This is where all riders are proceeding in a line, either abreast or ahead and turn off (or return to the line) one at a time. It is particularly useful for getting into or out of a wheel.

There are other movements which can be incorporated with the above, such as loops, serpentines, half-circles off the track and diagonals back, as well as the simpler connecting devices of lines and pairs. It is up to you to explore the possibilities.

Incidentally, no team can operate without a back-up crew. More of this in Chapter 7.

7

Demonstrations and Displays

While much of the information in this chapter could relate to any demonstration, it is becoming more popular to include musical pieces and you might find you are asked to perform when you have never been involved in such a venture.

Making a Decision

When the original invitation arrives, there will be a series of questions you will want to ask before you make your decision as to whether or not you will accept.

DESIRABILITY Do you want to do it at all? Is there a risk that your name will be forever linked to some cause of which you disapprove? Will it endanger your amateur status? Will it alter your horse's insurance status?

FEASABILITY Are you available on the specified dates? Have you a suitable horse or a team that will be ready to perform at that time? Is the venue within a reasonable distance?

REWARD What are the financial arrangements? That is, will there be a fee paid, expenses, percentage of take, nothing ('It's for charity!'). Are the rewards adequate? Do you care if they are not? Who pays for incidentals – programme printing, special props or costumes, the additional insurance premiums on your horse, copyright and entertainments licences? Who obtains those licences?

Logistics

Further questions arise once you have accepted the invitation, involving how you will go about things, and who does what. So the next step is to draw up a list of all the items that need to be considered and work your way through it. 'You' in this context is used in its plural form, for even if only one horse and rider is involved, she will need at least one other person to groom for her.

BACKUP Modern pop groups travel with a large team of people to look after their instruments, electronics equipment and costumes. These people are called 'Roadies' and the more complex the act, the more of them there are. The same applies to the musical ride, and if you are to produce satisfactory results in public, you will need to assemble your own roadies. With the exception of those who will actually handle the equine members of the team, they do not need to be horsey, so fathers and boyfriends can be roped in. What is important is that each one should have specific tasks to perform.

You will certainly need at least one groom, dresser and music player. You might also need a wardrobe mistress, props man, jump erector, programme printer, poster sticker, money man and various 'gofers' ('Go for my whip, go for a hoof-pick,' etc.).

The money man handles all the finances, from collecting the fee to paying for sequins. He might also man a stand for you if you have your own particular message to impart to the audience (such as 'Arab horses are best') or items to sell.

One person should deal with all aspects relating to the horses. Are their shoes all firm? Have they all got haynets for the journey? Is the tack all ready and is each horse ready dressed at the right time? Are there stables available for your use and, if so, who provides the bedding and mucks it out? Finally, if inoculation certificates are needed, this person should be responsible for collecting them, showing them to officials and returning them to their rightful owners.

Another person should deal with the wardrobe. Even if there are no actual costumes involved, riders will want to change into performance clothes when they are ready to ride.

This means changing facilities, or space in a horsebox, and some consideration for separating the sexes. A wise wardrobe mistress will carry an emergency kit with needles and thread, ribbons, hair nets and pins, spare ties, gloves and whips, and boot polish. She should also bring a large roll of sticky tape for last minute lint removal.

Someone should handle everything concerned with the venue. Shape and size of arena and gallery location should be checked well in advance, as you need to know this to finalise your choreography. How many complimentary tickets will there be for parents and friends of riders? What are the parking arrangements? How long will it take to get there?

What condition is the surface in? This is no minor point. Some places never rake their schools and have a deeply worn track round the outside; others never water them and they are so dusty that the audience will hardly see you from the far side and you will spend the next week getting the dust out of your horses' coats and your clothes, and half your team will have sore eyes. All of this can be avoided by an inspection and insistence that the surface should be damp and even.

Are there security arrangements which you must comply with? (e.g. The Royal Mews.) Will cameras and videos be allowed? If you do not wish to be videoed by strangers, can you prevent it?

Unless you have a very good eye for shapes and spaces, it is a good idea to organise some markers to line yourself up with. These could be cones or posts outside, or discreet markers on the walls indoors, or a handful of fresh shavings on the centre point of the floor. If it is to be the latter, don't omit to show it to the horses before the audience arrives.

Rehearsals

You must have at least one run through at the venue, to let the horses and your riders have a good look at the place. If any of the horses are not used to large numbers of observers, take the trouble to introduce them to this situation well in advance, by enlisting as many friends as you can (or the local Scouts) to come to a dress rehearsal. Make them applaud and take flash photos, too, or your final bow will be marred by frightened horses leaping backwards.

Also take the time to familiarise your riders with the geography of the venue, with simple maps if necessary. It is silly to keep the audience waiting because a rider can't find the toilet, or has taken her horse to the wrong door. Ideally there will be somewhere for your team to await their entrance out of sight of the audience, but if not and you want to retain the impact of costumes for the grand entry, you will need to organise some cloaks and attendants to remove them at the right moment.

Music

If you are asked to perform a display at a big public show, do not omit to ask, well in advance, how your music will be played. If it is to be from your own cassette, all will be well, but insist that it must be your cassette and ensure the organisers will not change that arrangement at the last minute. If there is a live orchestra to play the music, insist on speaking to the conductor or musical director and tell him exactly what speed you require and whether there are any specific 'cues' in the music on which you depend. Also insist on at least one ride through with the orchestra as a rehearsal, otherwise you may find out when you try to perform that they have made their own arrangement of the music and ruined all your careful planning. Better not to do it at all than to be made to look foolish in public.

For smaller occasions, take spare copies of your cassettes, all carefully labelled and all ready for the 'Play' button to be pressed. There should ideally be nothing else on the tape. Provide your own button presser and your own player with spare batteries in case something goes wrong with what's provided. It is surprising how often the built-in machine, which you have been assured is in good working order, refuses to function on the night.

If your performance involves more than one piece of music, each should be on a separate cassette. These should be labelled in such a way that it is clear not only in which order they should be played, but how many there should be. The simplest way is 'No 1 of 3'. If you can see the operator from the arena, you can nod or speak when you are ready for the next piece. If you can't see the operator, or you want your performance to be totally polished, you should provide a script which makes it quite clear when buttons should be pressed.

'Ballets'

In this context, this term covers all dramatic enactments of stories. Unless the story is a short one and the music is continuous, a more detailed script will be needed. The music controller will need a copy and you will you also need a stage manager and possibly a prompter, both also armed with scripts. The stage manager ensures new players make their entrances on time. The prompter will be difficult to situate, but perhaps he could function as a narrator. Then, if anyone does 'dry up' he can cover for them by narrating their part for them.

In any situation involving the spoken word, unless a member of your team has written the script, copyright permission must be obtained. Like music, copyright in dramatic scripts or other forms of the written word, lasts for 50 years from either the writer's death or later first publication. Even titles on their own are covered.

Programmes

If you are providing a team, there should be a printed programme, no matter how humble. It should list all the performers, all the roadies and, with ballets, details of the authors and adaptors. A brief résumé of the storyline never does any harm.

List the music used, in order, and give details of the musicians. If you are using a piece composed for you or it is played by a live musician, there should also be a brief resume of their career.

Do not forget to be lavish with mentions of any sponsors. As well as the usual people to be approached, it might, in this context, be worth asking the local record shop.

8

Costumes, Props and Scenery

Safety

The first and most important consideration when choosing costumes for a musical ride is safety. Unless all the horses and riders involved are old hands at public performances, either or both are bound to be nervous. Even are if the horses are used to strange places, lights, loudspeakers and a crowd, at least some of the riders will be anxious about forgetting their parts and that anxiety will transmit to the horses. Add noisy or flapping costumes or caparisons and you have the perfect recipe for disaster.

Whatever you settle for, first make sure that everything is secure enough to stay in its place. Then to make sure it does what you want it to, and to get the horses used to it, have a full dress rehearsal. This is essential, for two minutes before the performance is no time to find alterations are needed.

It is also no time to present your horse with what he believes is a dangerous stranger – and no joke having to blindfold him before he will let you mount. You may even have to dress in front of your horse a few times before he'll accept you. Don't forget that if he is used to seeing you in tight trousers and with your hair in a net, you will be a completely different shape in a full skirt, a long wig, or a clown's outfit. If you have compounded it by smelling strange as well (greasepaint, spray paint, etc.) you must be even more patient.

Accustom your horse to seeing you in costume

Comfort

Don't assume that you will only have your costume on for ten minutes and that you can tolerate a little discomfort for that long. Murphy's Law says that you will be delayed before performing or be needed later for the Grand Parade. If you are too hot (and don't forget that lights at indoor shows generate a lot of heat, as does the crowd) you will soon become red and sweaty. Your makeup will run, maybe staining your costume indelibly and you will get sore from your costume rubbing damp skin.

If you are uncomfortable, you will be tense and that is not conducive to a relaxed performance. So, keep costumes lightweight if at all possible and loose enough to allow some air to circulate. Certainly nothing should be so tight that it restricts your freedom of movement, or makes it difficult to mount.

Credibility and Visibility

Most of your audience will see most of your performance from quite a distance. It must be immediately obvious what you are supposed to be from the other side of the arena. Consider that St Trinians schoolgirl — maybe most girl's school uniform now consists of a skirt, shirt and tie, but that uniform could apply to many other situations. For this purpose, it has to be a gymslip, with black stockings and a hockey stick (tell your horse it is a new sort of schooling whip!). The hat must be battered felt and the tie should be worn with the knot under one ear. Hair should ideally be wired pigtails that stick out. With that lot, everyone will know immediately what you are and will settle down happily to watch a new version of a familiar story.

You almost have to be a caricature, where boldness of line is more important than details. Fine detail just won't be seen, so any decorations on costumes must be bold and obvious. If pompoms are called for, they must be big ones and in a completely contrasting colour to their background. If a military costume calls for a stripe down the trouser seam, it will need to be at least 3 cm wide.

Authenticity

Whatever type of costume you choose, you must either go for a vague stereotyped version, like a toy soldier, or complete authenticity, like the 1893 parade uniform of a captain of the Duke of Blankshire's 92nd Hussars. Military uniforms are so well documented that there is no excuse for getting them wrong. Murphy's Law says that one of the judges will have served in that particular regiment and be mortally offended if you have a single button out of place.

Any public library has a wide selection of books on costume, from basic books that cover 4,000 years in a hundred pages, to detailed studies of accessories such as shoes and reticules. Several publishers have costume series. Batsford has a ten part series called *Costume Reference* which starts at Roman Britain and ends with the 1970s. Blandford Press has several on *Costume and Fashion, Folk Costumes of the World* and lots on military uniforms. Bell and Hyman publish *Period Costume for Stage and Screen* by Jean Hunnisett, which covers women's dress from 1500 to 1800 and has lots of scale patterns. Hopefully, this will expand into a series. There are many more. If you want authentic military costumes, apart from trying your library, try model shops. There is a growing interest in war games and enthusiasts can buy blank models to paint themselves, so the shops stock booklets full of detail for them to copy. You could do a lot worse than to approach the regiment itself. Most regiments can trace their lineage even if amalgamation with another regiment has confused it somewhat; and most are usually keen to help. Contact the Imperial War Museum in London (see Useful Addresses) for help in locating regimental headquarters.

One snag with all this is that although there are plenty of books on costume and fashion and they are all lavishly illustrated, very few of those illustrations actually show horse riders. For this, you need paintings of riders. These are mostly equestrian portraits, which will be found in histories of noble families, or books showing paintings in stately homes. There is one book called *Horses in Art* by David Livingstone Learmouth, published in 1958. It is now out of print, so cannot be ordered from a bookshop, but your library will be able to get it for you through the reservation system.

Side-Saddle

For side-saddle wear, you need a copy of *The Saddle of Queens* by Lida Fleitmann Bloodgood (published by J. A. Allen & Company in 1959) which shows women riding from the fourteenth century. Do keep in mind that until hunting became an acceptable activity for ladies in the 1870s, all most of them did was tittup in the Park at the fashionable hour or ride very gently round the countryside near their homes. The society lady would have had a special riding habit (often a militaristic version of the fashions of the day) but the countrywoman would not have anything so elaborate.

The point about hunting is that as a result of its dangers, the modern side-saddle apron (which does not go under the rider's thighs or knees at all) was evolved. Before this, women wore voluminous skirts and petticoats to ride, and quite a few of them got dragged to their deaths when they fell off their horse and their skirts caught round the pommels.

There is no reason why you should not elect to put girls in ball-gowns for Viennese Waltzes. There is plenty of precedent in real life for putting them in wedding dresses too. But for safety's sake, no matter how full you want the skirts to be, do try to devise them like the modern apron, or as wrapovers fastened with Velcro so no-one can get dragged if they fall off.

Costumes

COWBOY COSTUMES This is always a popular theme and much of the cowboy music is suitable to ride to. The costume is easy to put together and comfortable to ride in, and there are groups of people all over the country who spend their free time enacting the Western cowboy lifestyle. They go to great pains to achieve authenticity and, as with all enthusiasts, they are usually willing to help others who express an interest in their hobby. Although comparatively few groups have horses, they will all know of those who do, and there you can check out all the gear and accoutrements. For total authenticity, do not forget that Western riding involves neck-reining.

HIRING COSTUMES At first thought, hiring costumes sounds like a good idea. The problem is that it is quite expensive (deposit plus a weekly fee) and it is not that easy to find a shop that has enough of what you want. With the recent revival of fancy dress parties, hire shops have sprung up in most towns, but most of them would be horrified if you told them you wanted to ride a horse in their stock-in-trade. Most of what they have is pretty basic and you could actually make it cheaper than hiring it. If you want a really elaborate costume and you are prepared to pay for it, go to a proper theatrical costumier in a big city. What they will all have, though, are such difficult items as swords, shields, crowns and policemen's helmets, and these cost very little to hire.

MAKING COSTUMES Assuming that you have someone on your backup team who can sew, making your own costumes is best. That way, you can have them exactly as you want, you can alter them if necessary, and no-one will fuss if you damage them. You could use a professional dressmaker, but she must not be afraid of horses as the final fitting will have to take place while the riders are mounted, and she must sit through a dress-rehearsal to see what adjustments are needed.

Before you start making costumes, try to visit an end of term exhibition at your local drama college and see how they have made their costumes and scenery. If you have never been back-stage, it will be a revelation, for they achieve amazing results with the most basic and crude materials.

One technique they use a lot is to make the costumes in cheap plain fabric and then give them colour and richness with paint. 'Lace trimmings' can easily be produced with car paint sprayed though a paper doily and elaborate 'embroidery' with more car paint sprayed through home-made cardboard stencils.

Cans of aerosol paint are available at most garages or branches of Halfords, and they come in an enormous range of colours, including gold and silver. Silver paint sprayed on knitted garments produces instant 'chain mail'. You can also get loose glitter powder and spray-on glue. Spray the glue through a stencil to produce a pattern and then shake the glitter over it for instant 'jewel encrusted' garments.

If you want to use real velvet or brocade, start with jumble sales where there might be old curtains. Or go to the haberdashery department of a large chain store and look at furnishing materials. Apart from the rich fabrics you need (rich in price, too, and heavy and hot to wear) they also stock cords and tassles to make epaulettes, jacket frogging and sabretaches.

Another stage technique you might like to adopt is that of one-piece garments. What looks like a jacket over a waistcoat over a frilly shirt (three garments — very hot) is actually false shirt and waistcoat fronts sewn onto the jacket. Unless you intend to wear them many times, there is not even any need for the jacket to be lined, and thus the whole outfit is cooler.

DRESSING HORSES   With period costumes you will need to dress the horses appropriately. Do study the old paintings to see how manes and tails were dressed and what sort of tack they used. On the whole, it is impracticable to think of having modern copies made of saddles and bridles, but you can at least try to use authentic looking girths and browbands, and not use Vulcanite bits. Saddle cloths and other caparisons can be decorated with spray paint, as can rein covers. If these are elaborately cut, paint will prevent them fraying and you won't have to hem them.

Hems of skirts and caparisons must be substantial if the garment is to hang properly and not flap. Curtain weights will not do — they do not look right and may frighten your horse if they bang against him. The only answer is the one used on side-saddle aprons — a hem 15 cm deep, with buckram inside if the fabric is lightweight.

If you are in medieval costume and want full caparisons for your horse, make sure they are not so long that they tangle around his legs, and leave them open in front so he can move properly. Give some careful thought to arrangements at the rear — if you feel they must be fitted and completely enclosed, allow room for some tail movement and go for dark colours with a waterproof lining or they will become soiled very quickly.

Props and Scenery

With props, the two main considerations are safety and dropability. Safety requires that items must not frighten horses, either by noise or sharpness; and must not be potentially dangerous to riders, whether the ones carrying them or the others. Anything that is liable to be dropped, especially at an embarrassing moment, must be fastened to rider or saddle. Garden twine is strong enough for the purpose and fine enough to be invisible to the audience.

To illustrate both these points, here is a story of Medieval Chivalrie which the author produced at a demonstration at the Royal Mews.

The Court came home from a hawking party (stuffed bird shapes attached to gloves) and went into the castle (painted on canvas attached to jump stands). The Princess and her handmaidens stayed outside to pick flowers (she stood still while they rode in circles to collect plastic flowers stuck to the walls with masking tape) until the Wicked Black Knight, mounted on a large dark brown cob (wearing caparisons made of a candlewick bedspread dyed black) dashed out of his castle and captured her. He dragged her back into his castle while the handmaidens galloped home screaming for White Knight.

He wore silver chain mail and a white surcoat, and his dapple grey wore a white sheet trimmed with silver. He rode to Black Knight's castle and challenged him by throwing down a gauntlet (silver paint on a motorcyclist's glove). Black Knight came out and they fought.

This battle had been the subject of much discussion and trial and error. At first it was thought Black Knight, being a complete rotter (everyone could see that, as he had a fearful moustache which he stroked in a nasty gloating manner) would have a Morning Star (spiked ball on a chain) but it was impossible to make one which would swing convincingly without being lethal. So both knights carried swords.

At first it was suggested that White Knight should knock his opponent off his horse, but that could have easily led to an injury and would anyway have meant a loose horse. In the end he knocked the sword from Black Knight's hand. White Knight's sword was attached to his scabbard by a long string, while Black Knight's was attached to his glove. This glove was loose unless the fingers were curled, and his sleeves were loose and long, so when it came to the time, he flung his arm back and straightened his fingers and the glove and sword flew off together. It looked as though his hand had been chopped off. He slunk off, nursing his 'stump' (to the boos of the crowd as he passed them) while our hero let the heroine out of durance vile and rode triumphantly round the ring with her. The music was an edited version of Fucik's *Wintersturmer*.

Going back to the scenery, the audience accepted it perfectly happily, despite the fact that the horses and riders could be seen clearly while inside their 'castle'. This is something that is difficult to accept until you have actually observed it, but if the story has caught their imagination, they will accept the crudest scenery. After all, Shakespeare often had no more than a sign saying 'A Wood outside Athens'.

The only other concern is that scenery should be easily transported and that the horses accept it happily.

9

Music as a Teaching Aid

Before considering the specific issue of music as a teaching aid and in which situations it is valuable, it is worth considering why it is valuable. To do this, we must first look at the mechanisms of learning, for its greatest value is with the novice rider.

We have already mentioned proprioception, as the innate human ability to locate oneself spatially. It does not just cover our ability to know where our whole body is in relation to outside objects, which is useful in judging speed and distance, it also covers our ability to locate each part of the body in relation to another part of the whole.

It is this ability that allows you to shut your eyes and unerringly touch your nose with a finger. You do not need to think about it, or adjust the finger's route to your nose — your brain knows full well where your nose is and has no difficulty in directing the finger to it.

But that particular movement is well within the range of muscular movements normally made by finger and arm. It is when you ask for an unusual movement that hesitation arises, or even an inability to obey. The newcomer to any physical skill, including horse riding, is asked to perform a number of unusual (to them) movements.

One of the classics here, which every riding teacher will have encountered, is the pupil who is told to put her lower leg back and fails to respond. Or rather, as far as the teacher is concerned, has failed to respond, for on repeating the in-

91

struction, the response will be 'But I have!' The pupil genuinely believes she has moved her leg back, but since she is unused to feeling it in that position at all, she cannot feel that it has not altered.

What the teacher should do in this situation is to take hold of the leg (gently!) and move it from where it was to where it is wanted several times, saying 'This is where it was, and this is where I want it when I say "Lower leg back"' each time, until the pupil can do it accurately on her own at the command.

What the teacher is doing here is helping the pupil to imprint the necessary sequence of muscular responses on her kinaesthetic memory, which is the brain's collection of 'how to perform this action' instructions. In future, the trigger phrase 'Lower leg back' will automatically trigger that response — until such time as another trigger takes over, such as the desire to perform a half-pass.

This is the important point. These triggers can be changed during the development of a skill. A piece or sequence of music can be used as a trigger until such time as it is no longer needed, when that set of human muscular movements have become the automatic response to the proprioceptive recognition of a change in the horse's movement pattern.

Two of the commonest problem areas with new riders are achieving rising trot, and sitting properly to the canter. The usual way to deal with the trot problem is to say 'One means up, Two means down. One Two, One Two, One Two'. The pupil then bumps round the school muttering 'One Two, One Two' hopefully, and every so often her count will coincide with the footfalls and she'll get it right. Eventually she gets it all together, but it is a slow and painful process, for her and the horse.

Now, if you get the right piece of music (that Monty Python music really is good for this) you can teach the horse to trot regularly to that music, every time he hears it. He'll soon get the message, and he'll slot his steps into the beat. Then you play the music to the pupil while she stands on her own feet and make her flex her knees to the beat. Finally you put her on the horse, play the music, and away they go. Most people get it in one session; few take more than two, but they all go home humming the music, which serves to reinforce the rhythm in their heads.

Once they have got rising trot established as an automatic response, you can dispense with the music. Until, that is, you want to introduce the concept of using the speed of the rise to control the speed of the trot. Then, with more pieces of trot music at different speeds, the message soon gets through.

The canter problem is partly one of failing to get the sequence of body movements right, and partly of failing to keep the horse in canter long enough for the rider to sort out that sequence in her head. Unless you have a good lunge horse and enough space to send the horse to the end of the lunge on a good big circle, you have to let the pupil loose in the school and hope the horse stays in canter. What mostly happens is that he strikes off coming out of a corner, then accelerates along the long side until the pupil panics at the fast-approaching corner and claps on the brakes, usually losing her balance in the process.

If you can provide a good steady piece of canter music and teach the horse that he canters evenly every time he hears it, your problem will be halfway solved. He will not accelerate from the transition and the pupil will have enough of her attention on the music to allay her fear of the corners. As above, you can later produce some varied tempo music (this is where those Viennese Waltzes are useful) to help show her that she can control the speed of the canter, and her fear of crashing into corners will be gone forever.

With pupils who are really nervous of any aspect of riding, you can do much to calm them down by playing soothing music, or to distract them by getting them to sing along. Conversely, you can gee-up the dozy pupil or idle horse by playing rousing music. And (dare one suggest this?), if you have a class lesson and can teach them no more with the available horses, there is a great deal you can do with the aid of music to ensure they go away happy, wanting to return for another session. If numbers allow, you can work your way through all the team patterns, and you may even find you have a usable demonstration team at the end!

Do not forget that you should hold the necessary licences if you intend to use music as a teaching aid.

Useful Addresses

Anglo-Austrian Society
46, Queen Anne's Gate, London SW1H 9AU

The Arts Council of Great Britain
105, Piccadilly, London W1V 0AU

British Academy of Songwriters, Composers and Authors
148, Charing Cross Road, London WC2

British Horse Society
British Equestrian Centre, Kenilworth, Worcs, CV8 2LR

Mrs Gaynor Colbourne (who will compose and play, or edit and prepare competition tapes)
2, Cripley Road, Farnborough, Hants, GU14 9PZ

Imperial War Museum
Lambeth Road, London SE1 6HZ

The Incorporated Society of Musicians
10, Stratford Place, London W1N 9AE

Mechanical Copyright Protection Society Ltd
41, Streatham High Road, London SW16 1ER

The Performing Right Society Ltd
  29–33 Berners Street, London W1P 4AA
  (Freephone Linkline Number 0345 581868)

Phonographic Performance Ltd
  Ganton House, 14–22 Ganton Street, London W1V 1LB

Riding Club Office
  British Horse Society (as above)

Side-Saddle Association
  Foxworth Farm, Stichins Hill, Leigh Sinton, Worcs

Readers of this book who wish to be informed about new and forthcoming publications on horses and horsemanship are invited to send their names and addresses to:

J. A. ALLEN & CO. LTD.,
1, Lower Grosvenor Place,
Buckingham Palace Road,
London, SW1W 0EL